KNOWLEDGE AND POWER
Science in World History

William E. Burns
George Washington University

PEARSON

Boston   Columbus   Indianapolis   New York   San Francisco   Upper Saddle River
Amsterdam   Cape Town   Dubai   London   Madrid   Milan   Munich   Paris
Montreal   Toronto   Delhi   Mexico City   Sao Paulo   Sydney
Hong Kong   Seoul   Singapore   Taipei   Tokyo

Executive Editor: Jeff Lasser
Editorial Project Manager: Rob DeGeorge
Editorial Assistant: Julia Feltus
Senior Marketing Manager: Maureen E. Prado Roberts
Marketing Assistant: Marissa O'Brien
Managing Editor: Central Publishing
Operations Specialist: Laura Messerly
Creative Art Director: Jayne Conte
Cover Designer: Suzanne Duda
Manager, Visual Research: Beth Brenzel
Manager, Rights and Permissions: Zina Arabia
Manager, Cover Visual Research & Permissions: Karen Sanatar
Full-Service Project Management: Mohinder Singh/Aptara®, Inc.
Cover Art: © The Metropolitan Museum of Art/Art Resource, N.Y.: Leaf from an Arabic translation of the *Materia Medica* of Dioscorides ("Preparation of Medicine from Honey"), dated 1224.
Composition: Aptara®, Inc.
Printer/Binder:/Cover Printer: Courier/Stoughton
Text Font: Palatino

Credits and acknowledgments borrowed from other sources and reproduced with permission in this textbook appear on appropriate page within text.

Library of Congress Cataloging-in-Publication Data
Burns, William E.
 Knowledge and power : science in world history/William E. Burns.
  p. cm.
 Includes bibliographical references and index.
 ISBN-13: 978-0-13-615561-4
 ISBN-10: 0-13-615561-8
 1. Science—History. I. Title.
 Q125.B949 2011
 509—dc22

                                                    2010040678

10 9 8 7 6 5 4 3 2 1

www.pearsonhighered.com

ISBN 10:   0-13-615561-8
ISBN 13: 978-0-13-615561-4

Dedicated to Evelyn

ontents

reword

The increasingly rapid pace and specialization of historical inquiry has created an ever-widening gap between professional publications and general surveys, especially surveys of world history. The purpose of *Connections: Key Themes in World History* is to bridge that gap by placing the latest research and debates on selected topics of global historical significance, as well as some of the evidence upon which historians base their insights, into a form and context that is comprehensible to students and general readers alike.

Connections focuses on specific issues of world historical significance from antiquity to the present, employing a combination of elements. They include: an introduction that places the issue into a broad historical perspective; four narrative chapters, each a case study of a significant aspect of that issue; primary sources relevant to each case study, accompanied by probing questions relating to the sources; and an epilogue ("Making Connections"), which offers further points to ponder.

Two pedagogical principles infuse this series. First, students master world history most easily if allowed to focus on specific themes and issues. Such themes, by their very specificity, as well as because of their general application, enable students to perceive and understand the overall patterns and meaning of our shared global past more clearly than is possible through reading, by itself, a massive world history textbook. Second, students learn best when asked to think critically about what they are studying. So far as the study of history is concerned, critical thinking necessarily involves analysis of primary sources.

To that end, we offer a series of brief, tightly focused books that embrace a radical simplicity and a provocative format. Each book goes to the heart of a key theme, phenomenon, or issue in world history—something that has connected humans across cultures, continents, and time spans. By actively engaging with this material, the reader comes to understand in a nuanced and meaningful manner how often distantly located human cultures have been connected to one another as key actors in the epic story of world history.

Alfred J. Andrea
Series Editor
Professor Emeritus of Medieval History
The University of Vermont

Series Editor's Preface

Visitors to Beijing are confronted by a wide variety of must-see historical and cultural monuments, and daily tens of thousands of them pour through the main gate of the Forbidden City and an equal number wander amidst the splendors of the Temple of Heaven complex, but very few, only a handful, ever visit one of the city's most venerable and important sites: the Beijing Ancient Observatory. Standing along the southeastern portion of the remnants of the Ming-era city walls, the observatory cannot be missed, as it rises 15 meters [nearly 50 feet] above the busy thoroughfare that runs by it, and numerous tour busses pass it as they race toward such nearby sites as Tiananmen Square. Hardly a bus stops to give its passengers even a glimpse of the observatory, which is now a museum. This is a shame on several levels. Construction of the observatory was begun in 1442, a scant twenty-one years after the Yongle Emperor (reign 1403–1424) moved the imperial court from Nanjing to what became Beijing (Northern Capital) and began the process of rebuilding the city into a fitting residence for the Son of Heaven. Given the centrality of astronomy and astrology in imperial China, whose emperor was charged

The Beijing Ancient Observatory and its Jesuit-inspired bronze instruments. (Alfred J. Andrea)

with maintaining a harmonic balance between earth and heaven, this was much more than a center for observing the movements of heavenly bodies. It was an essential department of state and a means through which the emperor and his family maintained the Mandate of Heaven. Beyond this fact, which should draw anyone who is at all interested in traditional Chinese cosmology, there are eight huge bronze instruments on the observational platform that are witnesses to an extraordinary period in Sino-Western relations.

As readers of this book will discover in Chapter 2, Jesuit missionaries to China played a key role in transmitting elements of Western science to the imperial court, including the nontelescopic, astronomical instruments that the Danish astronomer Tycho Brahe (1546–1601) had designed and used. Although he rejected Copernican heliocentrism, Brahe was the most accurate astronomical observer of his day, and the instruments he championed were superior to any that the Chinese possessed, even though China's astronomers had been constructing sophisticated devices for plotting the positions of stars and planets for well over a 1000 years.

Indeed, evidence exists of Chinese observations of such phenomena as eclipses as early as the second millennium BCE, and by the sixth century BCE, roughly the time of Confucius, the Chinese were maintaining detailed records of their astral observations. By the first century BCE, the Chinese had developed a rudimentary armillary sphere to calculate the movement and position of celestial bodies, and they continued to refine this instrument in succeeding centuries. The armillary sphere, which was a skeletonized device consisting of graduated metal circles (*armilla/ae* in Latin), apparently had been invented by the Hellenistic astronomer Hipparchus in the second century BCE, and in succeeding centuries it became a standard astronomical instrument across Eurasia and North Africa and was improved upon by Arab, Western European, and Chinese astral scientists. Records dated to 1090 show that the Chinese constructed a water-powered armillary sphere in Kaifeng, the Northern Song dynasty's capital city.

Given this millennia-long interest in the stars, some Chinese savants (but certainly not all) welcomed the astronomical knowledge from the West brought by the Jesuits. It was the Jesuits' good fortune—

A reproduction of an armillary sphere from 1439 in the courtyard of the Beijing Ancient Observatory. Initially constructed for and kept at this observatory, alongside the Jesuits' instruments, the original was moved to Purple Mountain Observatory at Nanjing in 1933. (Alfred J. Andrea)

and Chinese science's as well—that several emperors were among those who embraced this Western science. In 1669, the Kangxi Emperor (reign 1661–1722) appointed Father Ferdinand Verbiest, S. J. (1623–1688) as head of the Mathematical Board and director of the observatory. In these capacities, the Jesuit priest immediately took on the task of correcting the imperial calendar, which was of cardinal importance for the proper performance of the emperor's many rituals—rituals that maintained cosmological harmony. In order to carry out this task, Verbiest found it necessary to order the construction of six new astronomical instruments, all based on Tycho Brahe's designs. By 1674 they were finished, each fabricated by highly skilled Chinese bronze casters, and were placed on the observatory's platform alongside older Chinese instruments. In that year, he also published in sixteen volumes the *Xinzhi Lingtai Yixiang Zhi* (*A Report on the Newly Built Astronomical Instruments in the Observatory*), Mandarin being a language in which this Flemish Jesuit was fluent. In his detailed report, Verbiest described the purpose and function of each instrument, how each was to be employed, and how they could be replicated. In the years that followed, Verbiest's Jesuit successors, Kilian Stumpf (1655–1720), Ignaz Kögler (1680–1746), and August von Hallerstein (1703–1774), combined to add two more bronze instruments—a quadrant altazimuth (1714) and an armillary sphere (1744)—to complete the set of eight.

This Jesuit involvement in Chinese astronomy illustrates a major motif that runs throughout this excellent book: The transmission of scientific and technological knowledge—whether it be from the Greeks to the Arabs; the Arabs to the Latin West (Chapter 1); or the West to Russia, Japan, and Africa (Chapters 3 and 4)—is a dialogue between the transmitter and the receiver. In most cases, ideas, techniques, and instruments are not simply adopted, they are adapted to a host culture and thereby made comfortable for and acceptable to that host. Even when the relationship between the two entities is unequal, as in the case of colonial subjects, such as in the Americas and Africa (Chapters 2 and 4), the host culture invariably has an impact on the manner in which the knowledge and power of science and technology are given, received, and, in many cases, enriched and returned to the host culture.

The ebb and flow of history is never simple, and this is especially true when it comes to the history of science, despite the wrong-headed attempt of some to present it as a linear story in which good science progressively drives out bad science. What we have here is a book that in its nuanced analysis and clarity of presentation offers a complex, multifaceted story (or, better, collection of different stories) that, regardless of the complexity, can be easily followed. As such, it not only adds significantly to the overall excellence of the Connections series, but also capitivates any student of world history, no matter how learned or ignorant (as is the case with this series editor) she or he might be regarding science and its history within a global context.

Alfred J. Andrea
Series Editor

About the Author

William Burns is a historian living in Washington, DC. His previous books include *The Scientific Revolution* (2001), *An Age of Wonders: Prodigies, Politics and Providence in England, 1657–1727* (2002), *Science in the Enlightenment* (2003), and *Science and Technology in Colonial America* (2005).

Acknowledgments

A lot of work went into this book, not all of it mine. I would like to thank my editors, Al Andrea, Charles Cavaliere, and Rob De George. My understanding of world science has benefited from conversations with Paula Findlen, Nathan Sivin, Andrew Zimmerman, and Dane Kennedy. The following reviewers provided helpful suggestions during the writing and revision process: Robert Friedel, University of Maryland; Michelle Gherke, Glenville State College; Karen Oslund, Towson University; Anthony R. Santoro, Christopher Newport University; and Rick Warner, Wabash College.

I also appreciate the Institute of Jesuit Sources allowing the use of the excerpt from Matteo Ricci's *True Meaning of the Lord of Heaven* and Oxford University Press allowing the use of the excerpt from E. B. Worthington's *Science in Africa*.

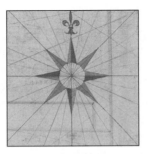

Introduction

On September 1, 1644, there was an eclipse of the Sun in China. It was a time of great uncertainty, given the fall of the Ming dynasty and its replacement by the Qing, the dynasty that had recently accomplished the "Great Enterprise" of conquering China. The Qing, who would rule China into the twentieth century, were originally the leaders of a people known as Manchus, from China's northeast, whom most Chinese would have perceived as barbarians. Like other Chinese departments of the Chinese government, the Astronomical Board, whose job it was to predict the time, extent, and duration of the eclipse, had to prove itself to its new masters. Predicting the precise time and duration was a difficult challenge. The calculations required were extremely complex and demanding.

The board had two branches calculating the eclipse, the traditional Chinese branch and another branch that used methods developed in the Islamic world. But there was a third entity making calculations, more foreigners, these from lands far to the west of China. The mysterious

"Black Robes," Jesuit missionaries from Europe, claimed both to know the only true religion and to possess superior methods of calculation. In their minds the stakes were even higher, as they hoped that accurate calculations would incline the new rulers' minds favorably to their religion. Their leader, Johann Adam Schall von Bell, known to the Chinese as Tang Ruowang, submitted a petition to the Manchu regent, Dorgon, accompanied by predictions of the eclipse. He asked that the Board test the accuracy of the Jesuits' predictions along with their own, a request Dorgon granted.

The great day arrived. The grand secretary, along with Schall von Bell and officials from the Astronomical Board, made their way to the observatory. The Jesuit calculations proved the most accurate, and Schall von Bell won what had always eluded the Jesuits in China, an appointment in the Chinese bureaucracy. He was the new head of the Astronomical Board, a position Jesuits would hold with one interruption until 1774.

That day in 1644 saw the coming together of three major scientific traditions, the Chinese, Islamic, and Western. It is one of the many cultural encounters and conflicts out of which the modern world of science has been created.

Twenty-first-century science is the product of millennia of human attempts in many cultures to understand the world that surrounds them and the bodies in which they live. This book explores several episodes in the history of science across the world.

WHAT IS SCIENCE?

The title of this book comes from a famous statement of the English Renaissance philosopher Francis Bacon (1561–1626), "Knowledge is Power." It is particularly appropriate for a study of science, for in few human activities are knowledge and power so intimately intertwined. Science has been both an attempt to understand the world and an attempt to master it.

The simplest definition of science, which derives from *scientia*, a Latin word meaning "knowledge," is that it is the study of nature. But that definition immediately raises a host of questions. What is nature? Are all kinds of study of it science, or does science coexist with other approaches? What is the relationship of scientific claims of knowledge to other claims, such as those of religion or of everyday experience? And, how does scientific knowledge relate to technology and other ways of not merely understanding nature, but using it to achieve human goals? Much science has been done with the eventual hope of "practical" use, not merely the acquisition of knowledge for its own sake. Every human society makes use of nature, but are all of these uses "science"?

The power science seeks has not always been simply power over nature. One of the themes of recent scholarship is that science cannot be severed from the social institutions in which it takes place, including those of power and domination. Science has been deeply marked by the quest for power over other societies and peoples. Scientifically advanced civilizations, particularly the modern West, have drawn on the power of their science to justify their claims to superiority in other areas of life. Science is also bound up in other power relationships. Men have used science to argue that their domination over women is a consequence of their innate biological advantages, and members of ruling classes have viewed their privileged positions as the product of the laws of nature.

SCIENCE AND THE SCIENCES

Science is divided into fields, or disciplines, such as physics or chemistry. Disciplines and the disciplinary structure themselves have a history. The discipline of natural history, for example, as practiced in ancient and early modern Europe, included botany, zoology, and mineralogy. Today, zoology and botany are on the opposite side of the line dividing the life sciences from geology. One characteristic of how science has developed, particularly in the twentieth and twenty-first centuries, is that the number of disciplines has increased as fields have divided and subdivided. Physics is now divided into nuclear physics, condensed-matter physics, cosmology, and a host of others, which in turn are divided into numerous subfields, and scientists have had to become increasingly specialized.

One area on the borderline of science is the so-called social sciences, such as sociology, economics, and anthropology. Not everyone agrees that these disciplines are sciences. However, since the eighteenth century, social, economic, and psychological thought has adopted many of the institutional trappings and methods of the sciences, including the quest for scientific law, quantification, and the use of controlled studies.

WHY DO SCIENCE? WHO DOES SCIENCE?

Today science is a profession employing millions of people through-out the world, but this has not been true until very recently in human history. For most of that time, science was practiced not by profes-sional scientists but by a variety of people, including clerics, physi-cians, and amateurs, whose interest in science was often ancillary to other concerns. A scientific profession emerged only in the nineteenth century, when the English word "scientist" was first coined.

In those civilizations with active scientific communities, practic-ing science has generally been easier for persons of higher social sta-tus, who have the leisure and resources for reflection and research. Until recently, a scientific career was extremely difficult for women, who had considerably less education and leisure time than men. It was also difficult for those born into the lower classes, for whom the daily demands of survival took precedence over research and speculation.

Scientists and others have practiced science for many reasons. One of the most basic is that science is fun. Many scientists, including some of the greatest, have practiced science and made important dis-coveries out of the sheer joy of it. This is not just true of the great sci-entists or even of people who would call themselves scientists. One characteristic of the last few centuries has been the rise of science as an activity for hobbyists and amateurs, who collect rocks, point their telescopes at the sky, and gather wild plants, as well as practice a myriad of other scientific pastimes. This type of science is restricted to those who have the wealth and leisure to engage in it or those who can make their scientific hobby pay.

Religious motivations have been important for many scientists, including Isaac Newton (1642–1727), sometimes claimed to be the greatest of all. The idea that science is a means of understanding the "mind of God" through understanding his creation is an old one. Another reason for people to practice science is because they thought it would be useful, on an individual or a social level. Success in sci-ence has led to social advance. Newton, the son of a small farmer, be-came one of England's most powerful and revered figures, buried in Westminster Abbey among the great of the land. Many scientists, par-ticularly in the twentieth and twenty-first centuries, have practiced science as a profession and sought advancement within its hierar-chies. The growth of the scientific profession has been one of the re-markable stories of the last two centuries.

Society has increasingly created scientific jobs for many reasons, from promoting economic development to proclaiming the glory of a ruler or a nation. Scientific knowledge has also promised to solve social and individual problems. Medicine and science have been closely interlinked for millennia, and much of the life sciences has been practiced with the hope of curing diseases. On the other side of the life/death equation, twentieth-century physics received a great deal of its support from militaries seeking more effective and destructive weapons. Not only states, but also private enterprises fund scientific inquiry to increase their profits or to develop new markets. For example, the petroleum industry and its endless need to locate and exploit new sources of fuel has employed thousands of geologists and deeply influenced modern geology.

IS SCIENCE WESTERN?

The physical world that science explores is the same "objective" reality for all human societies. But this does not mean that science simply floats above cultures. Human beings have been thinking and theorizing about the natural world we live in ever since there have been human beings, but not every society has interpreted science in the same way or even possessed a concept similar to "science." When science has emerged, it has been deeply shaped by the cultural environment in which it has been practiced. Cultures have influenced who does science, for whom they do science, and what sort of science they do. Different cultures have produced different sciences or scientific traditions, with different agendas, questions, and methods for answering them. Cultures have provided scientists with institutions and modes of communication and have set limits to the questions scientists can ask.

Scientific ideas also travel between cultures. In the last 1,000 years one particular scientific tradition—originating in the ancient Near East among the Egyptians and Mesopotamians, built upon by the ancient Greeks, transmitted to the Romans, expanded on in early Islamic society, and adopted by medieval Latin Christians—has become the dominant scientific tradition over the entire world, making science for the first time a truly global practice and institution. Scientists in Beijing, Addis Ababa, and Antarctica work with the same concepts, problems, and methods derived from this tradition—the tradition of "Western" science.

The classical discipline of the history of science, as it was formed in the late nineteenth and twentieth centuries, took Western science as the norm, and often viewed non-Western thought on the natural world either as not "science" at all, or as principally to be analyzed in terms of its failure to reach the heights that the West had achieved. This was part of a larger, "Eurocentric," historiographical tradition emphasizing the uniqueness and superiority of Western, or Euro-American, culture. Science, by its success, underlay Western preeminence. "Non-Western science," if not exactly a contradiction in terms, was a phenomenon of only minor interest. This position was not restricted to Westerners. Non-Westerners educated in the Western tradition were also likely to interpret their own history in terms of a failure to modernize, a narrative in which the inferiority or nonexistence of their science played a central role.

By the mid-twentieth century, this position had been successfully challenged on a number of fronts. English scholar Joseph Needham (1900–1995) established the power and range of classical Chinese scientific thought and creativity in a long series of works on science and technology in China. The importance of medieval Islamic science was explored by the Belgian-American historian George Sarton (1884–1956), and a number of scholars who followed him. The practices of hunter-gatherer, nomadic, and agricultural peoples, which are not identified with the major urban traditions of civilization, has increasingly been defined as a kind of science, although one that differs from the "high culture" scientific traditions by being set forth in practices and traditions rather than texts.

Once non-Western scientific traditions had been identified, their role in relation to Western science became an issue. Much early scholarship, on Islamic science in particular, was "contributionist," concerned with identifying specific "contributions" that non-Western science had made to Western science. Certainly such identifiable contributions exist. One example is the Hindu-Arabic numeral system, invented in India and reaching medieval Europe through the Islamic world. The superiority of the Hindu-Arabic system over the clumsy Roman numerals previously used was fundamental to the rise of science in the early modern period. However, a too heavy focus on contributions can lead to a shortchanging of those areas of non-Western science that are most different from Western science, as well as a reinforcement of the idea that the only important science is Western.

HOW DO SCIENTIFIC IDEAS MOVE
FROM CULTURE TO CULTURE?

There are many ways scientific ideas can travel between cultures. One is as part of a package, in which one culture adopts (and adapts to its indigenous traditions) the "high culture" of another, including science, along with its philosophy and literature, and often its religion. Two examples of this process are the Roman adoption and adaptation of Greek culture and science and the Japanese and Korean adoption/adaptation of the culture and science of classical China. Another process of adoption involves one culture picking and choosing from among the products of another. The medieval Islamic caliphate, interested in Greek science and philosophy, had little interest in Greek literature and religion. The Spanish Empire adopted new medicinal and food crops and the means of cultivating and preparing them from Native Americans, but it accepted little else from people whom the Spaniards believed needed to be converted, baptized, and civilized. Likewise, Japan's leaders in the nineteenth century selectively adopted Western science and technology to defend the empire against predatory Western powers.

A third kind of transfer occurs when one society essentially imposes its science on another. For example, nineteenth-century European administrators and teachers forced their own intellectual categories, such as European systems of numbering and classification, on the peoples they ruled.

WORLD SCIENCE AND THE SCIENCES OF THE WORLD

The world is not just a place where science is practiced; it is also a subject of science. The rise of global scientific networks has added vastly to the data available to scientists. The importance of the data varies greatly between different sciences. Some, like mathematics, physics, and inorganic chemistry, can be successfully practiced in isolation from the world outside the practitioner's own community. Others, like botany, zoology, and geology are immeasurably enriched by data gathered from global sources. Before the European discovery of Australia, the only marsupial, pouch-bearing animal known to science was the opossum of the Americas. The discovery of a wealth of marsupials, including kangaroos, koala bears, and Tasmanian devils in the new continent forced European zoologists to vastly expand their classifications, and raised important issues about the preservation in isolated environments, such as Australia, of forms of life extinct elsewhere. Some disciplines, such as geography and climatology, take the world itself for their subject. Even astronomy, whose subject matter exists outside the Earth, benefits immensely from accumulating a vast number of observations from as many different points of view on the Earth's surface as possible.

In the last few centuries, the scientist has been an integral part of numerous missions of exploration. Many of the most famous journeys, such as that of Lewis and Clark over the continent of North America or the voyages of Captain James Cook in the South Pacific, have been motivated by a desire to gather scientific knowledge, along with the ambition to claim new territories. One of the greatest scientific breakthroughs of all time, Charles Darwin's theory of evolution through natural selection, was in large part based on the observations he had made as a scientist on the round-the-world voyage of the British ship *Beagle*, a voyage in large part intended for scientific research. But voyages of exploration are often the preliminary, or sometimes the companion, of expeditions of conquest, and the scientist has been part of them as well.

Science and scientists have not just traveled through the world. In many places, from the North Pole to the South, science has also covered the world with a network of observation stations, from astronomical observatories and weather stations to seismological monitoring centers and experimental agricultural gardens and farms.

SCIENTIFIC INSTITUTIONS

Science is carried on not only by individual scientists, but also by scientific institutions. Institutions bring scientists together for projects that require more time, resources, and effort than one scientist can give, and they provide continuity over time for periods longer than a single scientific career. One of the most important aspects of the growth of science in the last millenium has been the creation, growth, and subdivision of the institutions in which science is done and communicated.

For much of the period covered by this book, the most important scientific institutions were educational establishments. Scientists who were not university professors often had to seek support from the rich and powerful (or sometimes, they were rich and powerful themselves). Science has played vastly different roles in different educational systems. In general, the tendency has been for science to become more important in education over the last few centuries.

Other important scientific organizations include scientific societies, with roots in the seventeenth century and an endless proliferation to the present day. By the eighteenth century, scientific societies could conceive and carry out projects embracing much of the world, such as coordinated astronomical observations and the collection of botanical and zoological data from many continents. Scientific societies also play an important role in "authenticating" the credentials of scientists.

Governments themselves have increasingly become the most important scientific institutions, employing hundreds of thousands of scientists and being the major funders of scientific research. Government agendas have shaped science, as eighteenth-century astronomy was shaped by the British and French governments' attempt to find a way to reckon longitude, and twentieth-century physics was shaped by weapons development.

WHAT IS THE HISTORY OF SCIENCE?

The history of science as a discipline has grown in the late twentieth century. Historians of science use a variety of different approaches. One important distinction, although many would regard it as oversimplified, is between the internal and external approaches. Internal approaches view science as shaped by human minds wrestling with the realities of nature. This can be done by focusing on the ideas and careers of "great men," such as Charles Darwin and Albert Einstein, or looking at the more pedestrian activities of ordinary scientists. The common thread of internalist explanations is that they locate the dynamic of scientific change within science itself. Internalists also tend to treat science itself as a cultural constant, an attempt to understand the physical world, done well or badly in different eras and societies. Internalist history of science was often practiced by persons with much more expertise in contemporary science than in the social, political, or cultural history of past societies outside of their science.

Most historians of science in the early to mid-twentieth century, when the history of science was establishing itself as a discipline, shared the values of scientists. The history of science in its early days was *teleological*—end oriented—tracing the emergence of more correct views and how they replaced less correct ones. (Another term for teleological history is "Whig" history.) Scientists of the past were valued in terms of how close they came to current ideas. The title of one popular survey of the history of science published in 1960 was *The Edge of Objectivity*. The author, Charles Gillispie, treated the history of science as a story of how discipline after discipline was subjected to "objective" thinking, and how since then each discipline, now "scientific," has progressed, becoming an increasingly accurate account of nature.

Early historians of science often focused on physics, seeing it as the model science and believing that other sciences aimed for the same structure as that of physics, a discipline characterized by laws expressed in mathematical form. This model privileged disciplines more amenable to mathematical analysis, and marginalized those, such as natural history, which were more driven by empirical fact gathering. It also tended to emphasize the few "great scientists" over the masses of ordinary working scientists.

Internalists trace the development of the ideas of great scientists according to their internal logic and scientists' engagement with the "mysteries of nature." When internalists do allow for social influences on science, they tend to blame bad science on social causes. For example, few would deny that the Roman Inquisition's 1633 trial and condemnation of Galileo Galilei for espousing Copernican astronomy was something outside science itself that had an impact on science. It set back the development of astronomy in Catholic societies by demonstrating the punishment awaiting Catholic astronomers who accepted the idea that the Earth orbits the Sun rather than the other way round. All internalists would admit that the trial affected science, but they would view it, and most social causation, as promoting bad science. Good science for internalists was usually promoted by scientists thinking about nature in a situation free of external constraints (although this glosses over the important question of how the money and the time necessary for scientific research are provided).

Externalist history of science tends to locate scientific change in changes to the society and culture in which science operates. There are several externalist approaches. Some historians relate changes in scientific thought to changes in the outside intellectual world, as do those who look at changes in religious and magical thought in the early modern period of European history to help explain the scientific developments of the time. Like the internalists, these externalists treat the history of science as fundamentally intellectual history, but place it into a wider intellectual context than they would have by simply focusing on science alone. Some externalist historians are institutionalists, looking at how specific kinds of scientific institutions—medieval universities, Islamic observatories, or state-sponsored translation efforts like those of the Abbasid Caliphate and Tokugawa Japan—have produced different kinds of science. They have examined how patrons of science—from individuals to foundations and governments—have shaped science by choosing which research programs and scientists to support. Another approach is biographical, showing how scientific discoveries have been related to the personal ambitions and career moves of individual scientists.

Other externalists relate science to social and political changes in the world outside the scientific community. How have social changes, such as the coming of capitalism or the rise and fall of colonialism, affected science? Some have used these concepts to explain the origins and success of the Darwinist theory of evolution through natural selection. They have connected it to social developments, including the rise of competitive capitalism in nineteenth-century England and the expansion of colonial empires with their accompanying racism. Others embed science in different national or regional cultures. Even though English and French scientists in the nineteenth century regarded each other as colleagues, knew of each other's ideas, and followed up on each other's work, were there differences between "English" and "French" science? And if so, what were these differences, and why did they exist?

Some internalists criticize externalism as ignoring how scientific theories are shaped by natural reality, while some externalists attack internalism for its denial of the importance of social and cultural forces. However, many contemporary historians of science would not place themselves in either school, believing that both internal and external factors have influenced the development of science. This book avoids either reductionist approach in favor of showing how science has actually developed in different historical settings. It focuses on four episodes in the history of world science from the Middle Ages to the mid-twentieth century.

WHY THE MEDIEVAL MEDITERRANEAN?

Modern science emerged from the contact and clash of the cultures bordering the Mediterranean Sea. In the east and northeast, the Byzantine Empire carried on the language and traditions of classical Greece with a Roman and Eastern Christian twist. In the south and southeast, Islamic states promoted a new Arabic culture and science, while drawing on classical Greek elements. In the north and northwest, Latin Christian societies, initially the most backward, gained from contacts with their rivals. Relations among these cultures ranged from violence, including the crusades, to trade and cultural transmission. The medieval Mediterranean offers a classic example of scientific interaction between and among distinct cultures.

Some historians have viewed Western science as emerging from an earlier body of ancient and medieval thought called "natural philosophy." Natural philosophers differed from modern scientists in that their work was much more closely tied to speculation about the meaning of the universe, and nature was studied as a collection of symbols and examples of moral and religious truths. Although science and philosophy are now considered different disciplines, much of what we now call science emerged historically as part of philosophy. The ancient Greeks who founded much of Western science, such as Aristotle, were philosophers before they were scientists, although they would not have recognized the distinction. In the Christian era, natural philosophy was also tied to natural theology, an attempt to use nature, God's creation, as a means of understanding God. A common metaphor in the Middle Ages and early modern period was that God revealed Himself in two books, the Bible and the universe. The idea of science as a fundamentally secular activity, still less one at "war" with religion, is a recent—and still controversial—innovation in the Western tradition. Although science and religion have not always dwelt together harmoniously, the idea of a "war between science and religion" vastly oversimplifies their complex relationship. Religious institutions and patronage supported many scientists before science became an autonomous profession. Medieval universities, which were the nurseries of Western science, were religious institutions.

The heritage of ancient Greek science was taken in by the Islamic world, and the new Greco-Arab science was in turn brought to Latin Europe. As we consider the medieval Mediterranean, a number of questions emerge. How were scientific ideas able to move among such diverse cultures—Byzantine, Islamic, and Western Christian—and languages—Greek, Arabic, and Latin? What kind of people were the carriers of these ideas? Which institutions transmitted and received them? What accounts for why certain cultures showed great interest in science at some periods and very little interest at others?

WHY THE JESUITS?

From the sixteenth to the eighteenth centuries, Western science, along with Western-centered empires, emerged from Europe to cover much of the world. In the forefront of much of this activity was a Roman Catholic religious order, the Society of Jesus, or Jesuits, founded by Ignatius Loyola in 1540. The Jesuits from the beginning appealed to the intellectual elite. As missionaries and educators, they disseminated scientific knowledge, gathered knowledge from indigenous peoples, and created the greatest network for scientific communication the world had ever seen.

Ironically, the Jesuits are not best known in relation to science for their worldwide network of communication and knowledge-gathering or for the books they published in languages from Chinese to Latin. Instead, they are best known as opponents of the Copernican system of astronomy, with the Sun at the center of the orbits of the planets. Jesuits in the sixteenth century supported the Ptolemaic system, with the Earth at the center and the Sun and planets circling around it. In the seventeenth century, Jesuits mostly switched to the Tychonic system, with the Sun circling the Earth and the other planets circling the Sun. Devoted to the intellectual authority of the Church, which opposed Copernicanism, Jesuits participated in the campaign against Galileo Galilei, which eventually led to his trial in 1633, condemnation, and house arrest, although they had been his allies earlier in his career. The trial of Galileo became a touchstone for people who have viewed science and religion as inherently in conflict, and much of the role of the Jesuits as promoters of science has consequently been forgotten.

The early modern Jesuits are one example of one of the most important forces in globalizing Western science—Christian missionary networks. Both Catholic and Protestant missionaries in the early modern and modern periods set up hospitals and schools as bases for evangelizing. Many missionaries came to regard Western science and medicine as one of the most important tools in their kit. The Jesuits in China set a precedent for this approach, although its success was decidedly limited.

The marvelously complex involvement of the Jesuits in early modern science lends itself to a number of significant questions. What were the purposes of Jesuit scientists, and how did they relate to their religious mission? How did other cultures react to the Jesuit efforts? How did Jesuit science relate to the growth of European power in the early modern world?

WHY TOKUGAWA JAPAN AND ROMANOV RUSSIA?

A common feature of the history of modern science is the adoption of Western scientific values and practices by non-Western societies. Two of the earliest societies to do this, Russia and Japan, offer strikingly contrasting patterns.

Russia under the Romanov dynasty of tsars adopted Western science as part of a state-driven process of "modernization." It had little preexisting scientific culture when Tsar Peter the Great mandated a "scientific revolution" at the end of the seventeenth century. The infrastructure of an eighteenth-century scientific culture—an academy, a scientific press, journals, and science education—was installed with remarkable rapidity. However, science in Russia remained for many decades a foreign transplant that appealed to only a handful of indigenous Russians. The Russian Academy was mainly staffed with Germans and other foreigners lured to Russia by the government, and few scientific publications appeared in the Russian language, even though it acquired a new technical vocabulary. The development of an indigenous Russian scientific community was a far slower process, one often delayed or troubled by the government's ambivalence to Western or scientific values. Here we must ask: How "successful" was Peter's attempt to transplant Western science to Russia? And what constituted "success"?

Japan from the early seventeenth to the mid-nineteenth century was united under the rule of the Tokugawa family of shoguns. Far from sharing Peter's enthusiasm for Westerners and things Western, the Japanese rulers viewed them as a potential threat that yet had a potential for usefulness. Japan offers a unique spectacle of scientific traditions being transmitted to a radically different culture without the direct participation of representatives of those alien traditions. Japan was "the closed country" which restricted foreign contact to small groups of Chinese and Dutch traders separated from the Japanese population, yet both Chinese and Western science spread through the country.

Japan offers a place to observe the interaction of these two important traditions of world science in a society that was neither Chinese nor Western and had essentially no direct contact with either. Without an opening for the immediate interaction of Western or Chinese scientists with Japanese society, the scientific ideas of these two cultures had, nevertheless, to be adopted and absorbed by Japanese intellectuals. Given this reality, we might well ask: What advantages and disadvantages did Western ideas have over competing intellectual forces in Tokugawa Japan? Further, what function did Western scientific ideas and their supporters play in Japanese society and politics? Indeed, can the roots of Japan's extraordinarily rapid and effective modernization in the later nineteenth century, after the shogunate's overthrow, be traced to the Tokugawa period?

WHY AFRICA IN THE AGE OF IMPERIALISM AND NATIONALISM?

Societies have not always freely adopted and adapted alien scientific traditions. Sometimes, science has been imposed by superior force. The spread of Western science was an integral part of Western colonialism in the nineteenth and twentieth centuries. European empires in the age of "high imperialism," from the late nineteenth to the early twentieth century, extended through Africa, Asia, Australia, and numerous Pacific islands.

Science both preceded and followed European power. One of the most dramatic episodes in the history of high imperialism is the so-called Scramble for Africa, in the late nineteenth century, when a continent, hitherto mostly independent, was divided between European powers in the course of a few decades. Focusing on Africa enables us to compare colonialism as practiced by several European powers, including Britain, France, Germany, and Belgium, as well as the responses of a diverse group of indigenous societies. The entry of Western science into Africa was particularly momentous, as the African interior had been largely unknown to Europeans before the nineteenth century.

Once the European empires were established, science became part of their machinery for colonial domination. Whereas the Russians and Japanese had been free to pick and choose which Western ideas appealed to them, Africans had no such choices. In the colonial regimes, Europeans were constituted as the discoverers and holders of scientific knowledge. Africans were its object. Indeed, African peoples became material for Western scientists to study. Thus, the science of anthropology developed along with colonial domination. However, Africans were not merely passive objects of science. They both contributed to and resisted European knowledge. Science, and resistance to it, played a role in the African nationalist movements that would eventually overthrow the colonial powers.

In this light, we should ask the following questions: How was science part of European colonial domination? How did colonial rulers promote science? What role did science play in colonial education systems? Did science provide a model for imperial rule? What alliances could African nationalists make with science? How did newly independent African states deal with science?

CHAPTER 1

Science in the Medieval Mediterranean

Today science is practiced across the globe, and communication between scientists in different countries is quick, particularly with the use of the Internet. Language barriers still exist, but are of much less importance than in any other time in human history, as English has become the international language of science. In the Middle Ages, the period roughly from the rise of Islam in the seventh century CE to the beginnings of European global expansion in the fifteenth century, scientific communication, like communication in general, was slow and often required expertise in two or even three languages. Scientific works were laboriously written and copied by hand, on media that were relatively rare and expensive. Out of the cultural matrix of the Mediterranean, however, modern science was formed in the contact between civilizations.

Barriers to scientific communication were not merely linguistic. They were also cultural and religious. The three principal civilizations of the medieval Mediterranean were the Latin Christians, the

Greek-speaking Byzantine Christians, and the Arabic-speaking Muslims. Each of the societies also had a Jewish population, *in* them but not *of* them. In order for science to cross into different civilizations, it had to overcome the hostility that often existed between them. The wars of the Byzantines and Arabs went back to the early days of Islam. The twelfth century, in which the earlier trickles of Greek and Arab learning to the Latin West began to swell to a flood, was also the period of the crusades and the Spanish Reconquista, the slow process by which Christians regained the peninsula they had largely lost to Muslim invaders after the first Muslim invasion in 711. An army of Latin Christians sacked the Greek capital, Constantinople, in 1204. However, there was some cooperation and even amity between Latin and Greek Christians. There was also a fair level of interchange and cooperation among Muslims, Jews, and Christians. So, even within this warring world, the transmission of knowledge continued.

The principal areas for the intellectual development of Western science and medicine in the Middle Ages were the Islamic world and, beginning in the late eleventh century, the Latin West. Both areas built on the tradition of ancient Greek natural philosophy and medicine. The ancient authors: Ptolemy in astronomy, astrology, and geography; Galen and Hippocrates in medicine; Euclid, Archimedes, and Apollonius in mathematics; and Aristotle (along with works falsely ascribed to him) in logic (or dialectic), biology, and natural philosophy underlay medieval Islamic and Latin Christian science.

CLASSICAL SCIENCE IN THE ISLAMIC WORLD

From the eighth to the tenth centuries, the dominant military and economic power in the Mediterranean world was the Islamic Caliphate. The initial Islamic invasions of the mid-seventh century had destroyed the Persian Empire and taken much of the Middle East, North Africa, and Egypt from the Greek-speaking Byzantine Empire. Stretching from the Pyrenees on the present-day border of France and Spain to the Pamir Mountains in Central Asia, the Caliphate was a space for an unprecedented mixing of global cultures, including scientific and mathematical traditions. Although the science produced in the Caliphate and its successor states and societies is often referred to as "Arab" or "Islamic," such designations oversimplify the complex mixture that was early medieval Middle Eastern society. Many practitioners were not of Arab descent, and Christians of various sects and Jews, as well as Muslims, participated in science. What universally characterized this science were the Arabic language and its foundations in the Greek tradition.

The areas conquered by the Caliphate in the Middle East possessed scientific traditions, although they were no longer nearly as active as they had been centuries earlier. The most important tradition was that of Greece, dating back to the sixth century BCE and building on the science of the Ancient Near East, particularly Mesopotamia and Egypt. The Greek tradition had strengths in several areas, including natural philosophy, mathematics, astronomy, and medicine. With the expansion of Greek culture following the conquests of Alexander the Great, Greek science had spread to the Middle East, where the city of Alexandria in Egypt became one of its major centers. Although the Romans had defeated the distant successors of Alexander and incorporated several of their kingdoms into the Roman Empire, the dominant culture and science of the Middle East remained Greek until well after the Islamic conquests.

The desire to explore and eventually expand this scientific tradition was driven by Islam itself, which endorsed the seeking of knowledge as a religious duty. Several of the reputed sayings of Muhammad, such as "Seek knowledge, though it be as far away as China," called upon Muslims to learn and investigate. Islamic religious obligations also raised specific scientific questions. Muslims are required to pray in the direction of Mecca, known as the *qibla*, which made ascertaining it urgent for Muslims wishing to worship. Many of the advances in trigonometry in Islamic culture were driven by the problem of determining the shortest distance between two points, Mecca and the position of the worshipper, on the surface of a spherical Earth. (The roundness of the Earth was common knowledge in both Islamic and Christian lands.) Muslims were also enjoined to pray five times a day at set times, which made timekeeping important. Eventually, timekeepers would be attached to mosques as permanent officials. Astronomers also determined the proper dates of holidays and the holy month of Ramadan on Islam's lunar calendar.

However, not all motives driving curiosity about the natural sciences were religious. Astrology was denounced by some Islamic

Astrolabe, from Baghdad c. 1130. *The Granger Collection, NY.*

religious authorities, who argued that belief in the power of the stars insulted God's omnipotence, but it still attracted great interest in the early centuries of Islam. Many astronomers also worked as astrologers, although the religious condemnation of astrology as a violation of the principle that only God can know the future helped keep astronomy and astrology as separate disciplines. Medicine was also an important secular discipline in early Islam, and many of the important Arabic philosophers and scientists were physicians by profession. Technology and engineering, used for building, navigation, irrigation, and numerous other necessary functions were also allied to science.

THE TRANSLATORS

A society wishing to explore an alien scientific tradition has two choices. It can learn the language that the science is written in or it can translate the alien scientific works into its own. The Romans had adopted the first strategy. Romans interested in Greek science learned Greek, and little advanced Greek science was translated into Latin. This meant that when knowledge of Greek was lost in much of the Latin West after the end of the Roman Empire in the West, so too was the knowledge of advanced science. The first translators in the Islamic world adopted the second strategy, fostering translation from Greek and other languages into Arabic and, in doing so, creating a new Arabic scientific vocabulary. (And indirectly, much of the Western scientific vocabulary as well.) The Arabs took pride in their tongue, which in the early days of the Islamic Empire was the language of the sacred book of Islam, the Quran, as well as of an established poetic tradition, but not yet of science. Arabic was particularly useful as an ecumenical language that transcended local regions because it was intimately connected with Islam. Rather than being translated into numerous languages, the Quran was (and is) thought authentic only in its original Arabic. Schools of Arabic have flourished throughout the Islamic world to the present day. Although many of the peoples incorporated into the Caliphate kept their own day-to-day languages, Arabic spread as a learned and religious language among the elite and among converts to Islam. Eventually, even Christian and Jewish writers within lands dominated by Muslims used it.

Whereas translations from Latin to Arabic were rare and had no particular importance for the history of science, ancient Greek thought shaped the Arabic intellectual world through the translations and other activities of the *Bayt al-Hikma*, the "House of Wisdom," founded in Baghdad by the Abbasid Caliph al-Mamun (reign 813–833) around the year 832. Initially an expansion of the caliphal library, the House of Wisdom drew upon the massive resources of the Abbasid Empire in scientific manuscripts and expertise, which an earlier caliph, al-Mansur (reign 754–775), had added to through gifts of Greek manuscripts from the Byzantine emperor. It was the initial center of a translating effort that brought hundreds of Greek philosophical, scientific, and medical texts and commentaries, as well as Syriac and Indian works, into Arabic. In addition to Ptolemy, Galen, and Aristotle, the geometer Euclid, the physician Hippocrates, and the botanist Dioscorides were all translated into Arabic, along with a voluminous mass of Greek commentaries on

Aristotle. The *Bayt al-Hikma* also was a center for making copies of the new translations, a very important task in a manuscript culture.

Much of the work of the *Bayt al-Hikma* and other early translation centers was done by members of a particular religious minority, the Assyrian Church of the East, the so-called Nestorian Christians. The Church of the East had split off from the Christian Churches of Constantinople and Rome over theological issues in the fifth century. As a persecuted religious minority within the Christian Roman Empire, they had a long-standing affinity for loyalty to tolerant non-Christian rulers, such as most of the early caliphs. The church had established ed- ucational institutions at the town of Nisibis (in present-day southeastern Turkey) under the pre-Islamic Sassanian Persian Empire, and its intel- lectual traditions continued into the Caliphate. Familiar with the Greek language yet holding no loyalty to the Byzantine Christian Empire, Nestorians were in an excellent position to lead the translation effort.

Not all the translations made into Arabic were traceable to the Greek tradition. India, which also bordered on the Caliphate, had a rich body of scientific texts. An astronomical work was translated from Sanskrit to Arabic as early as 732. Although Arab scientists and physicians ultimately preferred to build on Greek rather than Indian scientific traditions, Arab, and eventually Western, mathematics and science benefited immeasurably from the adoption, improvement, and standardization of the Indian system of decimal numerals. The Indian numerals were far easier to use than previous numbering sys- tems, such as Roman numerals or the Greek use of letters of the alphabet for numerals. The new system, known to the Arabs as "Hindu," became known in the West as "Arabic." Some Indian arithmetic, such as elements of what al-Khwarizmi (died ca. 850), a mathematician who worked at the House of Wisdom, called *al-Jabr* (algebra), were also imported into the Islamic world, and eventually absorbed into the mainstream of Islamic mathematics.

FROM GREEK TO ISLAMIC SCIENCE

Baghdad had been transformed in 762 into the capital of a new dynasty of caliphs, the Abbasids, who came to power in 750. As the Caliphate established itself, it adopted a more eastern orientation, toward Persia and Central Asia and away from the Mediterranean. The eastern ori- entation was followed by the government's losing control over its western territories. In the tenth century, new rival Islamic Caliphates were established in Egypt and Spain. Following the Abbasid precedent, the Fatimids of Egypt and the Umayyads of Spain also viewed the patronage of learning and translation as part of their cultural programs. They established massive manuscript libraries in their capitals of Cairo and Cordoba. This westward diffusion would be particularly important in making Arabic science available to Western Europeans.

Sciences drawn from the ancient Greek and other pre- and non-Islamic traditions were known as "foreign sciences" or "ancient sciences." They were distinguished from the "Islamic sciences," which included such studies as Sharia (Islamic law), quranic interpretation, Arabic grammar, and similar disciplines. Islamic sciences always had far more institutional support and cultural prestige than the ancient sciences.

Medieval Islamic thinkers, notably Ibn Sina (980–1037) and Ibn Rushd (1128–1198), known in the West as Avicenna and Averroes respectively, further developed and systematized Greek thought, as well as introduced innovations. Ibn Sina and Ibn Rushd were both physicians, a common career choice for scientists in the Islamic world. Areas in which thinkers in Islamic-dominated areas (who included Muslims, Jews, and Christians) were able to significantly advance on the Greeks included mathematics, optics, and astronomy. Arab astronomers had the most sophisticated astronomical theories and techniques in the medieval world, as well as the most accurate body of astronomical observations available in the West before the late sixteenth century. Astronomical observatories—towers and associated buildings with a good location for viewing the stars, and possessing a variety of expensive astronomical equipment—were themselves an Islamic invention. The first was the observatory at Baghdad, built by al-Mamun around 828. It became common for rich rulers in the Muslim world to found observatories and sometimes to take an interest in astronomy themselves. Among the greatest of these was the observatory founded by the Mongol il-khans of Persia at Maragha in 1259, which brought together the leading astronomers of the Islamic world and a library of manuscripts looted when the Mongols had taken Baghdad and other major Islamic centers. Islamic astronomers became increasingly conscious of the flaws and contradictions in Ptolemaic astronomy and made many innovations within the Ptolemaic system, while not challenging the Earth-centered universe of Ptolemy and the majority of other Greek astronomers and natural philosophers. The superiority of

Islamic astronomy was recognized by other civilizations; not only did the Latin Westerners eagerly acquire Arabic treatises, but the Chinese Empire established an "Islamic department" within the Bureau of Astronomy. As late as the eighteenth century, the Indian Hindu ruler Jai Singh was building an observatory on the Islamic model.

The Arabs, notably al-Kindi (died 873), one of the earliest scholars associated with the Baghdad House of Wisdom, and the astronomer, mathematician, and religious scholar Ibn al-Haytham (965–1040), known in the West as Alhazen, also went far beyond the Greeks in optics, mechanics, and mathematics. (Al-Haytham was the first to describe a camera obscura.) Much of the modern mathematical vocabulary is derived from Arabic, including "algebra" and "algorithm." The term "algebra" comes from the title of a book by Muhammad Ibn Musa al-Khwarizmi, *Al-Kitab al-muhtasar fi hishb al-gabr wa-l-muqabala* (*The Compendious Book on Calculation by Completion and Balancing*), written around 820. With their development of algebra, Arabic mathematicians broke with the Greek tradition, in which the dominant element in mathematics was geometry, and laid the foundation for modern mathematics.

GREEK AND ARAB MEDICINE

Medicine was greatly developed by Islamic practitioners and theorists. There was a medicine indigenous to Islam, the so-called "Medicine of the Prophet." This was a systematization of quranic verses and hadiths, or sayings ascribed to Muhammad and his Companions, that related to medical issues. The Medicine of the Prophet was the first text studied by Muslim medical students, but it dealt with a limited range of issues, such as recommending cold water for fevers, and did not provide a theoretical framework.

This gap was filled by translations from the Greek and, to a lesser extent, the Indian medical traditions. In medicine, early Arabic writers (many of them Christian) built on the medicine of Jundishapur, a medical center in southwestern Iran established by the pre-Islamic Sassanian rulers of Persia in the sixth century CE. In this city, Greek, Persian, and Indian medical traditions met. Jundishapur was not at first greatly affected by the Islamic conquests, but dwindled as the Abbasid caliphs drew more of the leading physicians to their new capital at Baghdad. Choices made by the Arab translators would influence the development of medical theory in both the Islamic and Latin worlds for centuries.

Galenism, founded by the second century CE Greek physician Galen, had been only one of several competing schools of medical thought in the Roman Empire, but by translating over a hundred Galenic texts into Arabic, the House of Wisdom ensured it would dominate medicine in the Islamic world and eventually in the West for centuries. Although the Arabs did not initiate a new theoretical framework for medicine, they made great advances in pharmacology and surgery. Medieval Islamic civilization also developed physicians who were among the leading philosophers of their time, whether Muslims like Ibn Rushd or Ibn Sina or Jews like Moses Maimonides (1138–1204). Arabic-speaking physicians pioneered the creation of systematic compendia of medicine. Ibn Sina's *Canon of Medicine* was the most complete and best organized treatment of Galenic medicine available anywhere, and became the standard medical text in both the Islamic and Latin Christian worlds.

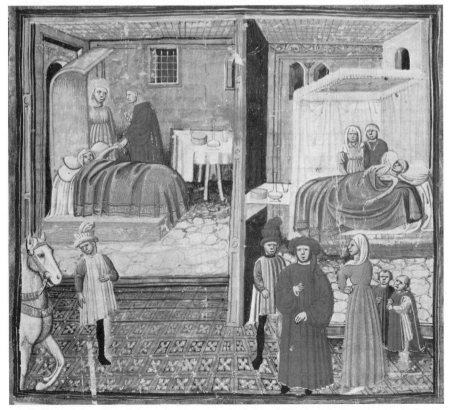

"The Doctor's Visit," from Ibn Sina's *Canon. Biblioteca Universitaria, Bologna, Italy/Scala/Art Resource, NY.*

GRECO-ARAB SCIENCE IN THE MEDIEVAL LATIN WEST

The Latin West in the early Middle Ages (ca. 600–1000) was too poor and rural to produce significant science and theoretical medicine. After most of Latin Europe lost the ability to read Greek, what was left was the Bible in Latin translation, biblical commentaries that dealt with natural science, and a few copies of the voluminous but unsystematic and uncreative Latin works of Roman and a few early medieval compilers, such as Pliny the Elder's *Natural History* or the encyclopedic writings of Isidore of Seville (died 636). What little investigation did take place was driven by religious considerations. Like Islam, Christianity posed some technical problems that led to scientific investigation. The problem of fixing the date of Easter attracted many of Europe's leading minds and led to the development of a form of calendar reckoning known as the "Computus." However, these efforts did not extend to an interest in science in general outside religious applications.

The revival of Western science can be traced to the growing prosperity of the West in the eleventh century. New technologies increased agricultural production. The age of barbarian invasions finally ended with the conversion of the last barbarian invaders, the Magyars from Central Asia who settled in Hungary and the Vikings of Scandinavia. More people had the time and leisure to explore scientific matters. Ancient Roman and early medieval writings in Latin were read in monasteries and taught in "cathedral schools," the dominant institutions of higher education before the rise of the university in the late twelfth century. The curriculum of the cathedral schools was dominated by the Seven Liberal Arts, a grouping of arts and sciences handed down from antiquity. They were "liberal" because they befitted a free man or *liber homo*. The liberal arts consisted of the *trivium* (the place where three roads meet), Latin grammar, rhetoric, and logic, and the *quadrivium* (the place where four roads intersect), arithmetic, geometry, astronomy, and music—the last treated as a theoretical and mathematical science.

Although the teaching of the Seven Liberal Arts in the eleventh century and for most of the twelfth century was based on some rather elementary Latin texts from Greco-Roman antiquity, these works whetted the appetite for more serious treatments of the natural world. These were available mostly in Greek or Arabic. Like the Arabs before them, medieval Europeans chose to acquire this learning in translation rather than by learning new languages. (In the thirteenth and fourteenth centuries, the great universities established chairs of Greek, Arabic, and other languages but these were largely for missionary purposes rather than the study of Greek and Arabic works.) An influx of translations from the Arabic began late in the eleventh century. These translations included both Greek texts previously translated into Arabic and original Arabic writings. However, the wide geographical expanse of the Islamic world affected which Islamic scientists became known in Latin Europe, as the works of not all Islamic scholars were equally accessible to Westerners. One of the greatest Islamic scholars, the geographer and physicist al-Biruni (973–1048), who worked in Persia, India, and the eastern lands of Islam, far away from the western Mediterranean, was not translated or known to European scholars at all.

The initial centers of translation were the frontier zones where Latin Christian culture intermingled with Greek and Arab culture. Of the three major zones where Christians and Muslims came into contact—Spain, the kingdom of Sicily and southern Italy, and the crusader states of the Middle East—virtually no intellectual exchanges took place in the crusader states. Christian-Muslim relations there were on a more constant war footing than in the other two, and the marginal economy prevented the development of an intelligentsia. Few intellectuals went to the Middle East, and many of the warriors and pilgrims who went there left after a few months (if they survived) and never developed an interest in the local culture or languages. There were more direct contacts between Latin society and Arabic science at the Palermo court of the Norman and Hohenstaufen kings of Sicily, Christian kings who adopted many practices of Islamic rulers. The great Arab geographer al-Idrisi (died ca. 1165/66) composed the *Book of Roger*, a geographical treatise, for King Roger II of Sicily (reign 1130–1154). Moreover, the area had also never lost its connections to Greek culture, and it consequently became the center of direct translations into Latin from Greek. These initially, however, had less impact on Western Christendom as a whole than works translated from Arabic.

The principal avenue for scientific translation from the Arabic was Spain, where many Islamic areas with developed scientific traditions were coming under Christian rule as Christian armies won back the peninsula they had largely lost centuries ago. This brought Christians into closer contact with the libraries and instrument collections

Islamic scholars had built, as well as with Islamic and other Arabic-speaking scientists themselves. The knowledge of the Arabs was supported by some Christian rulers, most notably the thirteenth-century King Alfonso X of Castile and León (reign 1252–1284), known as Alfonso the Wise or Alfonso the Astronomer. Alfonso's Alfonsine tables of astronomical motions were based on the work of the Spanish-Arab astronomer and geographer Abu Ishaq Ibrahim al-Zarqali (1028–1087), known in the West as Arzachel.

The beginnings of translation from the Arabic did not see a Western ruler step into the shoes of the caliphs and sponsor a program or institution dedicated to translation. Not even Roger II was a systematic patron of translations. Instead, translation was a more individual effort. The translators were an essential group of cultural intermediaries. Some came from the culturally intermediate community of Spanish Mozarabs, Christians living under Islamic rule who had adopted the Arabic language in their ceremonies. Another intermediate community was that of Jewish converts to Christianity. The most important translator of the twelfth century, however, came from neither group. This was Gerard of Cremona (1114–1187), whose life and work paralleled and stimulated the rise of Europe's first universities. Gerard was an Italian who worked in Toledo, Spain. Gerard's translations into Latin included over 70 Arabic versions of Greek works included Ptolemy's *Almagest*, Euclid's *Geometry*, and Archimedes's *Measurement of the Circle*. Arab originals he translated included Ibn Sina's *Canon of Medicine* and the commentary on Galen by Ali ibn Ridwan (known as Haly Abenrudian in the West), both of which became standard medical texts, as well as dozens of other books. The twelfth and thirteenth-century discovery of these Greek and Arab writers had a radical impact on European culture, making the physical universe an object of scholarly interest.

NEW KNOWLEDGE, NEW INSTITUTIONS—
THE RISE OF THE UNIVERSITY

The movement of scientific ideas between cultures is often facilitated by, or creates, new institutions, such as the *Bayt al-Hikma*. In Latin Christendom during the late twelfth and thirteenth centuries, the newly created "university" (from the Latin *universitas*, "a collective body") became the vehicle for disseminating science and medical theory. The new ideas coming from the Muslim world were not the only or even the most important factors in the creation of the university—the ever-growing need of church and state for theologians and lawyers played at least as great a role—but the undergraduate "Arts" Faculty and the Medical Faculty, one of the four (theology, canon law, civil [Roman] law, and medicine) graduate faculties, were fundamentally shaped by the new knowledge that provided a great deal of its curriculum.

The new universities were part of the growth of new institutions in high medieval Europe (ca. 1000–1350). Like town governments, universities had a permanent institutional existence guaranteed by charters. The first universities originated in Bologna and Paris sometime in the twelfth century. They and the numerous universities that followed were church institutions, entrance to which was restricted to male Latin Christians who enjoyed clerical status by virtue of being students at these institutions. This exclusivity helped give Latin Christian science a different character from the science of the Islamic world. Islamic science, reflecting the diversity of Islamic culture, was practiced by Jews, Christians, and Muslims, few of whom had any special religious status, but with the exception of a few Jewish physicians, science in the Latin Christian world was practiced exclusively by Latin Christians, most of whom were either physicians or affiliated with the church as members of the "clergy." As a result, Latin Christian science was more tightly integrated into its religious culture than Islamic science, although some religious leaders viewed it with skepticism.

The general faculty of the university whose masters taught the undergraduate community was known as the Arts Faculty. The Arts Faculty offered the Master of Arts, the basic undergraduate terminal degree, which gave the recipient a license to teach the Arts.

The bachelor's degree was instituted for those who stopped before completing the Master's program. The Master's degree was required of students going on to attain a professional degree in one of the four higher faculties. The primary mode of teaching in the Arts Faculty was the lecture, a "reading," during which the master read and commented on a text. In the course of the thirteenth century, Latin grammar and rhetoric were largely relegated to the preuniversity level, while the University Arts curriculum became increasingly based on Aristotelian philosophy, especially dialectic, or logic, the art of rational inquiry and analysis. The mathematical sciences of the quadrivium were also somewhat marginalized, although they continued to be taught to those interested, often outside the university classroom. Logic flourished and became an immensely powerful and complicated system ultimately based on Aristotle and the "syllogism," a way of arranging propositions from premises to conclusion.

The professors who taught in these universities are referred to today as "Scholastics" (from the Latin *scholasticus*, or teacher) because they were the first group of intellectuals in the West to be primarily employed as teachers. Scholastics did not view the understanding of the natural world as a discipline divorced from philosophy but as a subdiscipline within philosophy, "natural philosophy." Natural philosophy was taught in universities principally by commenting on Aristotle's genuine and spurious scientific works, along with received commentaries on these works and other ancient and Islamic texts. Aristotelian natural philosophy dealt with many questions now part of the discipline of physics. They included the nature of matter and the universe, the causes of motion, and the difference between the earthly and the celestial realm. Aristotelianism had the advantage of being the most complete system of natural philosophy available. However, it was not entirely satisfactory. Aristotle's thought had been produced in the culture of pagan Greece. Many aspects of it, most notably the belief Aristotle shared with other Greek thinkers that the world had existed from eternity and would continue to exist through eternity, were incompatible with Christianity. (Other aspects, like Aristotle's belief that the heavens were perfect and the Earth corrupt, and his notion of God as the Unmoved Mover were much more Christian-friendly.) Like Islam, Christianity had a central belief in a God who had created the universe at a specific moment and would destroy it. However, only a minority viewed the contradictions between Aristotelianism and Christianity as a fatal objection to all of Aristotle's philosophy. University Arts and theology professors faced the difficult task of reconciling Aristotelian natural philosophy with Christianity. The most common approach was simply to subordinate Aristotle to Christian doctrine. Scholastic thinkers denied that the world had always existed, and then tried to patch the hole this made in the Aristotelian system as best as they could. Some even pointed out that it would have been possible for God to have created a world that eternally existed, even though he had not done so.

A very different strategy for reconciling Aristotle and Christian tradition based itself on the philosophical works of the Andalusian-Arab

Ibn Rushd, "Averroes." Ibn Rushd was actually more influential in the Latin world, where he was known as "the Commentator" for his commentaries on Aristotle, than he had been in his own Islamic community. He was a great admirer of Aristotle, believing that in him the human mind had reached perfection and that there was no flaw in his philosophy. Ibn Rushd had asserted the autonomy of natural philosophy from Islam, and the Latin Averroists, such as the Paris Professor Siger of Brabant (ca. 1240–1284), followed him by asserting the autonomy of philosophy, including natural philosophy, from Christian theology. What exactly this meant was unclear. Averroists were sometimes described as believers in a "double truth," that what could be treated as true in doing natural philosophy could be treated as false in doing theology, but there is no surviving evidence of anyone openly holding this doctrine.

Along with the infiltration of Aristotle's texts and ideas into the universities came opposition from conservative church authorities, around the middle of the thirteenth century, and their concerted effort to use the church's authority to limit the permissible areas of study. This reaction evolved from the early opposition of conservative monastic leaders, including Peter Damian (died 1072) and Bernard of Clairvaux (died 1153), both well-educated, highly influential men who had led attacks on the application of logic, or rational analysis, to church doctrine and the Christian faith. The rise of Latin Averroism only made this project more urgent. Conservative theologians were also concerned that the Arts Faculty's use of philosophy was causing it to encroach on the territory of the Theology Faculty. The power of Aristotle's ideas and their usefulness to theologians, however, made a complete ban impossible. Instead, church authorities concerned about the conflict between Aristotle and Christianity concentrated their fire on certain specific ideas.

The flash point of this controversy was the University of Paris, the leading Arts and Theology university of Europe. The Paris theologians implored the bishop of Paris, Etienne Tempier (died 1279), to do something to preserve the university from the threat of the new ideas. Tempier reacted to the perceived danger of the Averroists by condemning many Aristotelian ideas as irreligious, first in 1270, and then much more sweepingly in 1277. The second ban was actually in response to the orders of Pope John XXI (Pope 1276–1277).

Two hundred and nineteen articles were condemned in 1277, some of them having little to do with natural philosophy or even with

"Studying the Heavens," from *De Natura Rerum* (Things of Nature) by Saint Albertus Magnus. *Picture Desk Inc./Kobal Collections.*

the university curriculum. However, the heart of the condemnation was directed at strong Aristotelians and "Averroists" and their alleged refusal to accept the truths of the Faith. This went beyond single doctrines like the eternity of the world, into the area of how the universe was governed. Could God act in contradiction to the physical principles defined by Aristotelian natural philosophy? Aristotelians believed in a single universe, or world. This in itself was uncontroversial, but some theologians believed that natural philosophers denied that it was possible for God to create multiple worlds. The condemnation of 1277 forbade this denial as an affront to God's omnipotence. The scope of Tempier's condemnation reached beyond the Averroists to many philosophers and scientists trying to synthesize Aristotle with Christianity.

The effect of this condemnation was limited, however. It did not stop the study of nature, nor was it intended to. It did encourage a greater focus on God's omnipotence, with a greater willingness to discuss hypothetical, non-Aristotelian cosmologies. These discussions were not assertions of physical reality, but remained speculative.

When the fourteenth-century Parisian master Nicolas Oresme, for example, discussed the anti-Aristotelian idea that the Earth rotated, his influential arguments were directed at demonstrating that it was possible, or at least impossible to disprove, not that it was actually happening. Other natural philosophers theorized about motion in a void, an impossibility for Aristotle.

The condemnation of 1277 also did not stop the use of natural philosophy by the Theology Faculty in discussing creation and other religious questions. University theologians, all of whom would have studied natural philosophy as Arts students, attracted criticism from authorities, including popes, for an overemphasis on natural philosophy and logic, as opposed to biblical interpretation in their work. In contrast to the Islamic world, however, where theologians and natural philosophers had little to do with each other, in Christian Europe theology and natural philosophy continued to be carried on by the same people or at least at the same institutions.

MEDICINE IN THE MEDIEVAL UNIVERSITY

Professional healing in early medieval Europe was not based on mastery of textual sources. The transmission of the Greek and Arab written tradition in medicine to Latin Europe only began in the late eleventh century, with a group of translations from the Arabic associated with the Italian Benedictine monastery of Monte Cassino. These translations, made by an otherwise unknown monk named Constantine the African, included the ancient Greek physicians Hippocrates and Galen, as well as Arab physicians. These new texts were instrumental in re-creating medicine as a learned profession, as well as ensuring that Western medicine followed Arabic medicine in adopting a basically Galenic framework.

With the development of the university system in the thirteenth century, medicine was taught alongside canon and civil law and theology as one of the four higher disciplines. The first important medical schools originated in Mediterranean areas, where Latin, Greek, and Arabic cultures and medical traditions met: Salerno in southern Italy and Montpellier in southern France. The legendary founding of Salerno, by a Jew, an Arab, a Latin, and a Greek, indicates its ability to draw on multiple medical traditions. As they did in science, universities benefited in medicine from the flood of Spanish Arabic translations of the mid-twelfth century, the most influential work being Ibn Sina's *Canon of Medicine*. A third wave of medical translations in the thirteenth century was led by the royal physician Arnauld of Villanova (ca. 1238–1310) and included a higher proportion of translations directly from the Greek. Latin Christians also began to write medical treatises, commentaries, and compendia of their own, although nothing as yet to challenge the intellectual authority of Greek and Arabic works.

The Bachelor of Medicine degree took about seven years, the MD (Medicinae Doctor) about ten. As the medical curriculum developed, textual study began to be supplemented with other forms of medical education. Some universities required medical students to get practical experience working with a physician, and beginning in the fourteenth century, some Mediterranean universities began to require attendance at dissections. (The bodies dissected were usually those of executed criminals.) The authority of medical texts, however, continued to reign supreme, and university-trained physicians made little effort to supplement or challenge textual authority with their own research and observation.

The Galenic medicine taught in the universities was based on a theory of the four "humors" of the human body: yellow bile, black bile, phlegm, and blood. A healthy body was one in which the humors were balanced. This led to the popularity of blood-letting as a therapy, as it allegedly relieved the distress caused by an excess of blood. Although Galen differed from Aristotle on some biological questions, Galenic medicine was mostly compatible with Aristotelian natural philosophy, and physicians were educated in natural philosophy as well as medicine proper.

ALCHEMY AND OTHER "DISREPUTABLE" SCIENCES— OUTSIDE THE UNIVERSITY

Not all Arab and Greco-Arab science found a place in the university. Some disciplines, notably experimental science, alchemy, and astrology were held in suspicion for one reason or another, often the taint of magic or heresy. However, practitioners of these sciences probably did not view them as magical. Excluded from the university curriculum, these sciences found homes elsewhere, notably the courts of princes.

University science, with the partial exception of medicine, tended to be "theoretical" and not oriented to practical uses. The medieval university had little interest in experiment, which had a disreputable association with magic. Some university masters might have experimented, but experimentation was not part of the curriculum. The experimentalist's "manipulation" of nature was often difficult to distinguish from that performed by magicians with demonic aid. The ascription of "natural" powers to items, such as magnets, was thought to verge on idolatry. These powers were often referred to as "occult," which in the Middle Ages did not refer to those powers which were magical, but those whose causes were hidden (*occulta*, "secret things," in Latin). The concept of "occult" science also includes the idea that knowledge of these effective sciences should be kept hidden from those who would misuse them. While natural knowledge was openly taught in the university, many works of occult science treated the transmission of knowledge as clandestine, using false names for the authors and codes and exhortations to the reader not to tell anyone of the secrets contained within.

The most important medieval experimental science was alchemy, a precursor of chemistry. Alchemy covered a wide range of intellectual endeavors, including the famous "Great Work," the search for the philosopher's stone capable of transforming base metals, such as lead, into precious ones, such as gold. Alchemy was also viewed in a spiritual sense, as a means of purifying the soul by purifying matter. Finally, there was also a medical alchemy dedicated to identifying chemicals that could cure disease and promote health. Many alchemists were also physicians. Western alchemy had Greek roots but had been developed by Arabic-speakers—the word "alchemy" first appears in Arabic, although there are different theories as to from where it came into the language. Knowledge of alchemy seems to have been lost in the medieval West along with the rest of Greek science. The first Arabic treatise on alchemy was translated into Latin in 1144. Much of the Western chemical vocabulary still bears traces of its Arabic origin—words such as alkali, naptha, alkahest, and alcohol. Learned alchemy as practiced in both Islam and the West demanded a familiarity with philosophy, often including Aristotelian matter theory. The most important experimental scientist of the medieval Latin West, the English Franciscan friar Roger Bacon (ca. 1214–1292), was also a university professor well-versed in Aristotelianism. His efforts to introduce alchemy and other experimental sciences to the university curriculum failed, however, and he later acquired the reputation of an arch-magician.

Alchemy was vulnerable to criticism on two fronts. The alchemical project of creating gold was viewed as fraudulent or demonic. Alchemical fraud was indeed common, as numerous charlatans claimed the ability to create gold, harming the reputation of the science. Laws were promulgated against them. "Spiritual" alchemy was denigrated for its association with mystical and heretical religion. Using alchemy to draw closer to God bypassed the sacred texts and institutional hierarchies of both Christianity and Islam.

In their suspicion of "magical" and experimental science, Christian religious authorities had much in common with their Islamic counterparts. Islamic alchemy had led a largely underground existence, often associated with heterodox forms of Sufism—Islamic mysticism. Although many Sufis were quite orthodox in their obedience to Sharia, Islamic authorities were suspicious of radical Sufis' emphasis on closeness to God through contemplation rather than following the law. Some of the principal Arabic alchemical texts were the creation of a mysterious and secretive sect known as the "Brethren of Purity," which apparently began in tenth-century Basra in Iraq and whose members probably constituted a minority Shia sect. The greatest of the Islamic alchemists, the even more shadowy Jeber ibn Hayyan, had been, according to tradition, a Sufi mystic. Work ascribed to him under the name Gebar passed into the body of Western alchemical texts. As was the case with the Brethren and Jeber, many works in ancient Greek, Islamic, and Western alchemy were anonymous or ascribed to legendary or fictitious characters. Moreover, improved communications across Eurasia brought about by the spread of Islam meant that Islamic alchemists were able to draw on Chinese Daoist ideas, such as the philosopher's stone and the elixir of life, ideas that were, in turn, passed on to the Latin West.

Alchemists also differed from mainstream Scholastics in their future-orientation—while the Scholastics usually presented their work in terms of the recovery of ancient wisdom, alchemists sometimes boasted that their science showed how the works of nature would be perfected by human art, another aspect of their science that aroused religious suspicion.

A key role in both the creation and transmission of alchemical knowledge was played by Jews. The association between Jews and alchemy went back to its earliest days—the first Western alchemist whose name is recorded is Maria the Jewess, who lived around the second or third centuries CE and was credited with the invention of a number of chemical tools and procedures, some still in use today. None of her writings survive, but she is mentioned in the oldest surviving Western alchemy texts, the fourth-century writings of Zosimus of Panopolis. Later writers identified her with Miriam, the sister of Moses. The strong continuing associations of Jews and alchemy can be seen not only in the careers of Jewish alchemists but the use of Hebrew as a language of power in alchemical texts. Both Ibn Sina and Vincent of Beauvais (ca. 1190–1264?), one of the most prominent thirteenth-century Christian alchemists and a Dominican priest, claim to have learned the art from Jewish masters. Jews who converted to Christianity, sincerely or insincerely, were also transmitters of alchemical knowledge to the Christian community.

A natural home for alchemists who claimed the ability to create precious metal was the court. Rulers had both the financial resources to supply alchemists with the materials they needed and a burning desire for wealth. Some alchemical writers warned against associations with princes, who would ceaselessly pressure the alchemist for gold, but a serious alchemical lab was expensive, and many had no choice but to seek financial backing.

Another "disreputable" science was astrology. Medieval astrology was based on the idea that the stars and planets exert an influence on the affairs of Earth. This influence was not necessarily "magical"; it was the enemies of astrology who associated it with magic. Many astrologers seem to have viewed the celestial forces as "natural." The knowledge of astrology, which had attracted the interest of Latin writers, as well as Greek, had never been entirely lost in the West. However, the era of translation greatly changed Western astrology, transforming it into a learned discipline. Arab writers had introduced many innovations into the astrology they had inherited from the Greeks and the ancient civilizations of Mesopotamia, Egypt, and Persia. Arabic works on astrology were translated into Latin, along with the writings and charts of Greek astrologers.

Astrology raised fundamental religious questions. It was opposed by both Christian and Islamic authorities because the idea that the influence of the stars determined events on Earth seemed to infringe on the omnipotence of God. Christians further attacked astrology on the grounds that it deprived humans of free will. Some also feared that astrology would lead to the worship of the stars and planets as gods. The general idea that the stars influenced events on Earth was accepted—it was undeniable that the Sun influenced the weather and the Sun and moon the tides—but many wanted to restrict astrology to general questions like weather prediction. Scholastic philosophers and physicians were willing to admit that the stars influenced the body, but were careful to specify that they could not determine a person's actions—the will remained free, even if a person chose to follow the promptings of the stars.

Like the alchemist, the astrologer was a "court" rather than a university figure. The principal job of the court astrologer was not to predict the future but, as was also true for court astrologers in China, to determine the right times for events. The position of the stars in the heavens determined the favorability of the time for royal enterprises, including coronations, military expeditions, medical procedures, weddings, and even the consummation of marriages. Court astrology also posed its dangers—one of the most severe astrological offenses was predicting the day of a king's death. This information was much in demand, particularly by rebels and other enemies of the ruler.

THE MISSING PIECE—WAS THERE A BYZANTINE SCIENCE?

Both Arabs and Latins drew on the heritage of ancient Greek science. The irony was that both far excelled the Greeks of their own day scientifically. The Orthodox Christian Empire of Byzantium, with its capital at Constantinople and directly descended from the late Roman Empire, survived in one form or another until 1453. Its language and civilization was Greek, but with many late Roman and "Middle Eastern" influences and components. The Byzantines started with many advantages in the study of science. Their knowledge of the Greek language was supported by what was by a considerable margin the greatest collection of ancient Greek manuscripts available anywhere. While the Byzantines faithfully preserved scientific and mathematical texts, and made enormous use of the pre-Christian classical heritage in areas outside of science, for most of their history they added almost nothing to the natural philosophy and mathematics of the ancients.

The one exception to the Byzantine nonproductiveness in science was the earliest phase of the history of this essentially neo-Greek empire as a separate entity from the Latin Empire of the West. From the fourth to the sixth century, Byzantium produced some important scientists, including the anti-Aristotelian physicist and commentator John Philoponus (ca. 490–570), who influenced subsequent Islamic and Latin science. However, these natural philosophers in retrospect seem more like the last of the classical Greek scientists than the founders of a new tradition. The empire lost Alexandria in Egypt, Philoponus's home and the traditional center of Greek intellectual life for nearly a millennium, to the Muslims in 642, a heavy, perhaps fatal, blow to the nascent Byzantine scientific tradition.

Byzantine access to the entire surviving Greek scientific tradition may have been paradoxically a handicap to the development of science. The overwhelming presence of the philosophers and scientists of classical antiquity to learned Byzantines seems to have produced a feeling that everything had already been said, and modern scholars could only quarry the works of the ancients rather than developing anything of their own. The Byzantines also possessed, unlike the Muslims, a powerful, centralized church that was often unfriendly to science. The Platonic Academy of Athens, considered with some reason to be a stronghold of the last pagans, was closed in 529 by Emperor Justinian. The church condemned an eleventh-century philosophy professor, John Italos, for an excessive love of classical, pagan Greek thought that had led to heresy. Condemned at the patriarchal church of Hagia Sophia in 1082 and shut away in a monastery, John the Italian (he was from formerly Byzantine southern Italy) was accused of believing in the eternity of matter and such Neo-Platonic ideas as the preexistence of souls and their transmigration. His condemnation was repeated in the service for the first Sunday in Lent for centuries. The Byzantine Orthodox Church never found the interest in science that the Latin Church developed in the Middle Ages. Although the Byzantines were aware of their backwardness in science and translated Arabic scientific texts into Greek, these translations did not spark the scientific revival in Byzantium that they did in the West.

THE DECLINE OF ARAB SCIENCE IN EARLY MODERN EUROPE

The early modern period, from roughly 1450 to 1700, saw a widening cultural gap between Latin Christians and the Islamic world, rapid growth in Latin Christian science, and increasing cultural confidence on the part of Europeans. All of these developments led to a lower regard for Arab science.

The communication gap between Islamic and Western civilizations had been widening since the late Middle Ages. The last conti-
nental crusader state in the Middle East had fallen in 1291. With the
expansion and tightening of Christian control in Sicily and Spain, the
old contact zones, the fast dwindling Muslim populations in these
two regions of Mediterranean Europe were increasingly cut off from
the high culture of the Islamic world. The increasing repression and
eventual expulsion in 1492 of the Jewish community in Spain, many
of whom had functioned as intermediaries between Arabic and Latin
cultures, also raised the barriers. Arab scientists did not participate in
the scientific flowering of the Latin university and later European developments, as they did not read Latin and manifested no interest in
European science. The real impact of European science on the Islamic
world would be delayed until the eighteenth century, at a time when
European science had clearly established its superior range and ability to pose and answer questions about nature.

Although the Islamic allegiance of some Arabic scientists had always been a stumbling block for Europeans, it did not invalidate their
science, just as the paganism of Aristotle and other ancient Greeks did
not lead Latin Christians to reject their science. The reputation of
Arab scientists and philosophers fell not because of Christianity, but
because of the construction of a "Western tradition," an early version
of "Eurocentrism." This was the work of the new humanists of the
fourteenth and fifteenth centuries. The humanists were intellectuals,
largely outside the university system, who rediscovered, or reinter-
preted, many of the writings of the ancient Romans and Greeks. The
most important claim the humanists made about the history of science was that the Greeks were the supreme masters, and little or
nothing had been done since their time. This led humanists who were
interested in science to attack both the medieval Latin Scholastics and
the Arabs as misinterpreters of Greek thought. The Arabs in particular were "barbarians" who had sullied the purity of Greek science.
Sixteenth- and seventeenth-century scientific and philosophical de-
baters often presented themselves as purifying Greek truth from
Roman, Arab, and medieval scholastic corruption, and the Arabs, unlike the admired ancient Romans or even the Scholastics, many of
whom were saints and revered doctors of the church, could be insulted with impunity. There was even a partially successful drive to
purify scientific language of Arabic-derived words, as in the shift
from "alchemy," a word whose root is of uncertain origin but which

clearly incorporates the Arabic definite article *al* (the), to "chemia," and eventually to "chemistry." Humanistic physicians also claimed to reject the "Arab" pharmacopeia, which created "compound" remedies by mixing different ingredients, in favor of a purportedly ancient method of curing diseases by one-ingredient "simples." Even though ancient physicians had recommended compounds, humanists claimed that European remedies were better suited to European bodies than the "exotic" ingredients of Arab medicine.

The impetus for the translation of new Arabic manuscripts into Latin died out in the Renaissance. This led to losses for Western mathematics, as computational techniques locked away in Arabic manuscripts would be painstakingly rediscovered by European mathematicians unaware of their Arabic precursors.

The other element that led to the undervaluing of Arab science was the remarkable European scientific progress of the late sixteenth and seventeenth centuries, the era of the "Scientific Revolution." The period saw an unprecedented development of astronomy, physics, mathematics, and numerous other disciplines in the West, which left ancient and medieval science far behind. Not just the Arabs, but all earlier scientists were increasingly seen as historical figures, not colleagues with whom present-day scientists were engaged in a dialogue.

However, Arabic science did not disappear entirely from Western intellectual life. Since many classical Greek works of science survived only in Arabic translations, even the humanists had to grudgingly admit the importance of Arabic knowledge. The established structure and curriculum of the university world also contributed to an educational conservatism that stood in contrast to the new anti-Arabic science ideology of the humanists. Ibn Sina's *Canon of Medicine,* along with the work of the Persian physician, alchemist, and philosopher Abu Bakr Muhammad ibn Zakariya-Razi (865–925), known to the West as Rhazes, remained a central part of the medical curriculum at many Western universities through the seventeenth century.

WHY DID SCIENTIFIC LEADERSHIP MOVE TO LATIN CHRISTENDOM?

Two of the most important questions in the history of science are how and why scientific leadership moved from the Islamic world to medieval Europe. This phenomenon is often described as "the decline of

Islamic science," but this description is not necessarily accurate. A scientific tradition can decline in two ways. It can decline absolutely, losing its dynamism and power to come up with new problems and solutions. This was the case with ancient Greek science after the age of Ptolemy and Galen. Or it can decline relatively, continuing or even accelerating but being outpaced by other, more quickly developing scientific traditions. Some scholars have argued that the decline of Arabic science was only a relative decline compared to Western science, whereas others have argued that an absolute decline contributed to relative decline.

The question of the shift between Islamic and Latin science, therefore, can be divided into two separate groups of questions. One is that of Islamic science and decline. Did the science practiced in the Islamic world decline absolutely and, if so, why and over what period of time? The other group of questions relates to Latin science. Why did medieval Latin science advance to the point of forming the foundation of the Western scientific tradition, which would eclipse all others, including the Islamic? When did the "takeoff" of Latin science begin?

The evidence for the absolute decline of Islamic science rests on the fact that there are relatively few major Islamic scientists after the thirteenth century. The founding of scientific institutions, such as observatories, also declined, but more slowly. The last major observatory founded in the Islamic world was the short-lived sixteenth-century Ottoman observatory at Istanbul. However, our knowledge is incomplete, as numerous medieval scientific manuscripts in Arabic and Persian have been lost or remain unexamined by modern scholars.

One explanation for Islamic scientific decline that has mostly been rejected by modern scholars is the destruction caused by the Mongol conquest of Persia and Iraq in the thirteenth century. The area had known destructive wars before, and despite the Mongols' alien culture and religion, they became patrons of higher Islamic culture, including science, and eventually the western Mongols, including the il-khans of Persia, became Muslims themselves. It was a Mongol khan, Hulagu, who founded the observatory at Maragha, in Iran, whose astronomers, most notably Nasir al-Din Tusi (died 1274), reached the highest intellectual level in astronomy in the Islamic world or anywhere else in their time.

Another explanation is cultural, focusing on the element in Islamic religious thought which was hostile to "ancient sciences."

Unquestionably, some Islamic thinkers, most notably the Sufi and theologian Abu Hamid al-Ghazali (1058–1111), condemned all inquiry not based on the Quran and Islamic traditions. There is some evidence that Muslim scholars who pursued natural enquiries faced persecution. However, this was never true all over the Islamic world, and the political fragmentation of medieval Islam after the fall of the Caliphate meant it was possible for scholars facing persecution to move to other, more tolerant Islamic lands. Nor was there any religious entity in Islam with the papacy's centralized power to suppress heresy and dissent. The works of al-Ghazali were also limited primarily to Sunni Islam in their impact. Although the Sunni were by far the largest Islamic sect, the other major sect of Islam, the Shia, continued to study natural philosophy as a way of reaching God. Even in the Sunni world, philosophers and physicians, such as Ibn Rushd, who wrote a refutation of al-Ghazali, continued to practice science.

The evidence for the rise of Western science is much stronger than the evidence for the absolute decline of Islamic science. Islamic science clearly produced nothing like the European scientific revolution of the sixteenth and seventeenth centuries. Another path of inquiry therefore is into the advantages that Western science had over Islamic science. What were the social, cultural, and intellectual bases of the "takeoff" of European science that Islamic science did not possess?

One factor many historians have pointed to is the difference between the European university and the most important institution in medieval Islamic higher education, the madrasa. Madrasas seem to have originated in the tenth century, before Western universities, and they had a more exclusively religious curriculum. Whereas the Liberal Arts were a central part of the undergraduate course of studies at most European universities, madrasas were specifically dedicated to teaching "Islamic sciences." There are a few known exceptions, among them madrasas that taught medicine, but they were very rare. Although there were other institutional bases for support for science in the Islamic world, among them astronomical observatories (a medieval Islamic invention) and hospitals, none combined the scientific focus and institutional permanence of the European university. European universities, although affiliated with the church, also had an institutional identity and autonomy from religious authorities that madrasas, which were connected to mosques, lacked. This autonomy led to a social space for relatively free speculation on natural philosophy. Although universities were often conservative in their approach to natural philosophy, over 80 percent of the most important scientists of the Scientific Revolution had attended a university, and many were university professors.

In the Islamic world, natural-philosophical discussion and speculation often took place outside institutions, in informal circles of friends and students. The fear of alienating religious authorities meant that knowledge was often not publicly circulated, which led to difficulty in advancing science. Islamic scientists were often unaware of other scientists working on the same or similar problems. For example, the *Optics* of Ibn al-Haytham, one of the most important works in Islamic science, virtually disappeared for two centuries after it was written in the eleventh century. References to it only begin after the late thirteenth century, when a scientist at the Maragha Observatory, Abu Hasan Kamal al-Din, wrote a commentary on it. The advantage Europeans possessed in the ease of scientific communication would be further widened in the fifteenth century, when printing was introduced to Europe. Printing spread quickly and widely in Latin Christian societies, while ruling authorities in the Islamic world kept it banned or strictly limited until the nineteenth century.

Another difference was intellectual. While many Islamic scholars were suspicious of all natural explanations of phenomena as infringing on God's exclusive creative power, such attitudes were much rarer in Western Christendom, and never received the endorsement of church authorities. Mainstream Christian theology accepted the idea that God governed the universe through reason, rather than solely through the divine will. Some scholars have argued that as the growing number of conversions to Islam made Middle Eastern society more "Islamic," naturalistic explanations had decreasing cultural room to be expressed. Islamic and Jewish philosophers in the Islamic world generally seem to have expressed themselves in more guarded language by the twelfth century.

One specific advantage that European medical scientists had over their Islamic contemporaries was that the prohibition on dissection in the Islamic world was rigorously enforced, while religious opposition to dissection in Christendom never succeeded in stopping the practice. The suspicion of visual images characteristic of most Islamic cultures also meant that Islamic societies never developed the practice of scientific illustration to the heights that Latin Christians achieved, even before the coming of the printing press.

Another difference between Islamic and Latin science was that the flow of information between them was one-way. Medieval Latin thinkers were keenly interested in Islamic science. Although a few Islamic scholars were aware of the philosophical ferment taking place among Latin Christians, most Islamic scientists displayed little or no interest in what was going in the universities of Europe. The language of European learning, Latin, was one that few Muslims knew, and the general belief that the peoples of Christian Europe were ignorant barbarians militated against Muslims studying their science.

The third major scientific community of the medieval Mediterranean, the Jewish community, became aware of the rise of Latin Christian science in the thirteenth century. Jewish physicians translated Latin works, and some looked enviously on the systematic course of instruction offered by Latin medical schools, as opposed to the more informal training of the Islamic and Jewish medical traditions.

MEDIEVAL LATIN SCIENCE AND THE SCIENTIFIC REVOLUTION

The relation of medieval Latin science to the "Scientific Revolution" of the sixteenth and seventeenth centuries has been a hotly debated question among historians of science. The idea of a scientific revolution implies a sharp break with the previously existing body of science. Although the leaders of the early modern Scientific Revolution did not use the phrase "scientific revolution," many of them thought of what they were doing either as something totally new, or as the revival of one or another ancient Greek intellectual tradition that was previously eclipsed by the domination of scholastic Aristotelianism. Even Aristotelians like William Harvey (1578–1657), who discovered the circulation of the blood, associated themselves with the ancient Aristotle rather than the Aristotelianism of Arab commentators or medieval university professors. There were exceptions—the astronomer and physicist Johannes Kepler (1571–1630) wrote a commentary on the thirteenth-century optical theorist Witelo, and the late medieval Scholastic natural philosophy to which most early modern scientists were exposed during their university educations left traces in their mature thought.

Despite elements of continuity, the idea of a sharp break with medieval science persisted through the eighteenth and nineteenth centuries, when medieval science was caricatured as dogmatic Aristotelianism, and medieval medicine as dogmatic Galenism. Denigration of medieval science was particularly congenial to Protestants and anticlericals, who blamed its alleged sterility on the dead hand of the Catholic Church. Liberals framed the Renaissance, the Protestant Reformation, and the Scientific Revolution as one vast movement of emancipation from the Catholic Church.

This picture was seriously questioned in the early twentieth century by a devout and conservative French Catholic who was also a distinguished physicist, Pierre Duhem (1861–1916). In various writings on the history of science based on extensive primary research in what were then obscure manuscripts, Duhem claimed that the true scientific revolution took place not in the early modern period but in the late thirteenth century, with Tempier's condemnation of some Aristotelian ideas in 1277. The effect of this decree, according to Duhem, was to inspire a group of avant-garde scholars at the fourteenth-century University of Paris, notably Nicholas Oresme (1325?–1382) and Jean Buridan (1300?–after 1358), to devise a new, non-Aristotelian physics which eventually led to the physics of Galileo and Newton. This was a reversal of the usual way of looking at the history of the Catholic Church and science. Rather than preventing the advance of science with its ban, the church had actually fostered it by liberating scientists from the dead hand of dogmatic Aristotelianism. However, Duhem's rehabilitation of medieval science was limited to that of the Latin West. Concerned mainly to defend the scientific reputation of medieval Catholicism, he ignored or denigrated the role of Islamic science in the development of the Western scientific tradition.

The most notable innovation of the Paris scholars was the idea of "impetus," a quality of a moving body that kept it in motion. This differed from the Aristotelian theory that a body's motion was maintained by the medium in which it moved. Impetus theory, claimed Duhem, led directly to the mechanics of Galileo, which was not a sharp break with the past, but the continuous development of a fourteenth-century tradition. The humanist Aristotelianism of the Renaissance was actually a step backward, and Galileo's work was a triumphant revival of the new physics of the Parisians.

No serious historian of science today views the science of the Latin Middle Ages as dogmatic or sterile. However, Duhem's claims about the connection of medieval physics to the Scientific Revolution have not held up under scholarly examination. The brilliant work of the late medieval Parisians and Oxonians continued to be expressed in the form of commentaries on Aristotle's works. They modified the Aristotelian system rather than overthrowing it. Many of their claims remained speculative. When Oresme discussed the rotation of the Earth, his influential arguments were directed at demonstrating that it was possible, or at least impossible to disprove. Copernicus, on the other hand, wanted to demonstrate that the Earth actually did rotate. Galileo was acquainted with the ideas of late medieval physicists, but his key contribution to the overthrow of Aristotelian physics—insistence on mathematization—was not based on their work. The concept of inertia as developed in the scientific revolution is quite different from late medieval impetus.

What medieval science did clearly accomplish was the revival of interest in scientific questions in European intellectual life. Medieval natural philosophers, mostly connected with universities, translated and circulated Greek and Arabic scientific and mathematical material, and made innovations of their own. Medieval scientists also established the disciplinary framework within which early modern scientists worked. When the Scientific Revolution did arrive, it arrived in a society in which scientific issues already had a recognized intellectual and institutional place.

SOURCES

■ Arab Science Enters the Latin West: Adelard of Bath

The Englishman Adelard of Bath (died after 1142) was one of the earliest Westerners to study science and philosophy in Arab lands. He wrote several important works, including the first Western treatises on the abacus and astrolabe, a translation of the first thirteen books of Euclid, and translations of Arabic texts on astronomy and alchemy. One of his works, *Natural Questions*, deals with basic questions about the nature of the universe such as "What holds up the world?" and "Why is the ocean salty?" This work is written in Latin in the form of a dialogue between Adelard and his nephew, in which Adelard represents Arabic learning, and the nephew the new Latin learning of the Paris schools, which emphasized dialectic. The treatise proved quite influential and was even adapted into Hebrew by the thirteenth-century Jewish writer Berechiah ha-Nakdan.

According to Adelard, what were the disadvantages or weaknesses of contemporary Western thought and learning? What did Adelard see as the advantages of Arabic thought? France being at that time the land in which schools of Aristotelian logic or dialectic were most in evidence, was he fair to French thought?

The dialogue begins with Adelard's return to England from his studies with the Arabs. He finds English society corrupt and depraved.

———————————

Thereupon my friends said to me, "What do you think of doing, since you neither wish to adopt this moral depravity yourself, nor can you prevent it?" My reply was "to give myself up to oblivion, since oblivion is the only cure for evils that cannot be remedied; for he who gives heed to that which he hates in some sort endures that which he does not love." Thus, we argued that matter together, and then as we still had time left for talking, a certain nephew of mine, who had come along with the others, rather adding to the tangle than unraveling it, urged me to publish something fresh in the way of Arabian learning. As the rest agreed with him, I took in hand the treatise which follows: of its profitableness to its readers I am assured, but am doubtful whether it will give them pleasure. The present generation has this ingrained weakness, that it thinks that nothing discovered by the moderns is worthy to be received—the result of this is that if I wanted to publish anything of my own invention I should attribute it to someone else, and say, "Someone else said this, not I." Therefore (that I may not wholly be robbed of a hearing), it was a certain great man that discovered all my ideas, not I. But of this enough.

Since I have yielded to the request of my friends so far as to write something, it remains for you to give your judgment as to its correctness. About this point I would that I felt less anxiety, for there is no essay in the liberal arts, no matter how well-handled, to which you could not give a wider range. Grant me, therefore, your sympathy. I shall now proceed to give short answers to questions put by my nephew.

Here begins Adelard's treatise to his Nephew.

****

Adelard: You will remember, Nephew, how seven years ago when you were almost a child in the learning of the French, and I sent you along with the rest of my hearers to study with a man of high reputation, it was agreed between us that I should devote myself to the best of my ability to the study of Arabic, while you on your part were to acquire the inconsistencies of French ideas.

Nephew: I remember, and all the more because, when departing, you bound me under a solemn promise to be a diligent student of philosophy.

The result was that I applied myself with great diligence to this study. Whether what I have said is correct, the present occasion will give you an opportunity of discovering; since when you have often set them forth, I, as hearer only, have marked the opinions of the Saracens [Muslims], and many of them seem to me quite absurd; I shall, therefore, for a time cease to exercise this patience, and when you utter these views, shall attack them {using dialectic} where it seems good to me to do so.

To me it seems that you go too far in your praise of the Arabs, and show prejudice in your disparagement of the learning of our philosophers. Our reward will be that you will have gained some fruit of your toil; if you give good answers, and I make a good showing as your opponent, you will see that my promise has been well-kept.

Adelard: You perhaps take a little more on you than you ought; but as this arrangement will be profitable not only to you but to many others, I will pardon your forwardness, making however this one stipulation, that when I adduce something unfamiliar, people are to think not that I am putting forward an idea of my own, but am giving the views of the Arabs. If anything I say displeases the less educated, I do not want them to be displeased with me also: I know too well what is the fate which attends upon the teachers of the truth with the common herd, and consequently shall plead the case of the Arabs, not my own.

Nephew: Let it be as you will, provided nothing causes you to hold your peace.

Adelard: I think then that we should begin with lighter matters, and if here I fail to give you a reasonable account, you will know what to expect in more important subjects. Let us begin then at the bottom, and so proceed upwards. . . .

Adelard: It is a little difficult for you and me to argue about animals. I, with reason for my guide, have learned one thing from my Arab teachers, you, something different; dazzled by the outward show of authority you wear a head-stall. For what else should we call authority but a head-stall? Just as brute animals are led by the head-stall where one pleases, without seeing why or where they are being led, and only follow the halter by which they are held, so many of you, bound and fettered as you are by a low credulity, are led into danger by the authority of writers. Hence, certain people arrogating to themselves the title of authorities have employed an unbounded licence in writing, and this to such an extent that they have not hesitated to insinuate into men of low intellect the false instead of the true. Why should you not fill sheets of paper, aye, fill them on both sides, when today you can get readers who require no proof of sound judgment from you, and are satisfied merely with the name of a time-worn title? They do not understand that reason has been given to individuals that, with it as chief judge, distinction may be drawn between the true and the false.

Adelard of Bath and Berechiah ha-Nakdan, *Dodi Ve-Nechdi*, ed. and trans. H. Gollancz (London: Oxford University Press, 1920), 91–92, 98–99.

■ Ibn Rushd on Islam and Philosophy

Abul Walid Muhammad Ibn Rushd (1126–1198), known in the West as Averroes, was among the greatest of the philosopher-physicians of the medieval Islamic World. From Spain, in the far west of a world that Muslims knew as *Dar al-Islam* (the House of Islam), Ibn Rushd devoted his career to the reconciliation of Aristotelian philosophy and Islam. The superiority of Islamic learning and the suspect nature of philosophy had been vigorously reasserted by the theologian al-Ghazali (1058–1111), and Islamic philosophers were on the defensive. In this passage from *Kitab fasl al-maqal*, known in English as *On the Harmony of Religions and Philosophy*, Ibn Rushd defends philosophy and the study of nature and the ancients on Islamic grounds. Ibn Rushd's work would have surprisingly little influence on subsequent Islamic philosophers (possibly due to his marginal geographic position as well as the general decline of Islamic philosophy), but would greatly influence Jewish and Latin Christian philosophers and theologians.

As you read this, ask yourself how Ibn Rushd reconciles religion with scientific investigation. According to Ibn Rushd is scientific investigation simply a legitimate area of inquiry, or is it more than that? If the latter, what is it and why? According to Ibn Rushd, how should a pious Muslim deal with the philosophical offerings of those pagan thinkers who lived before the advent of Islam? Why?

We maintain that the business of philosophy is nothing other than to look into creation and to ponder over it in order to be guided to the Creator—in other words, to look into the meaning of existence. For the knowledge of creation leads to the cognizance of the Creator, through the knowledge of the created. The more perfect becomes the knowledge of creation, the more perfect becomes the knowledge of the Creator. The Law[1] encourages and exhorts us to observe creation. Thus, it is clear that this is to be taken either as a religious injunction or as something approved by the Law. But the Law urges us to observe creation by means of reason and demands the knowledge thereof through reason. This is evident from different verses of the Quran. . . .

Now, it being established that the Law makes the observation and consideration of creation by reason obligatory—and consideration is nothing but to make explicit the implicit—this can only be done through reason. Thus we must look into creation with reason. Moreover, it is obvious that the observation which the Law approves and encourages must be of the most perfect type, performed with the most perfect kind of reasoning. As the Law emphasizes the knowledge of God and His creation by inference, it is incumbent on any who wish to know God and His whole creation by inference, to learn the kinds of inference. . . . This is impossible unless one possesses knowledge beforehand of the various kinds of reasoning and learns to distinguish between reasoning and what is not reasoning. This cannot be done except one knows its different parts, that is, the different kinds of premises. . . .

One cannot maintain that this kind of reasoning is an innovation in religion because it did not exist in the early days of Islam.[2] For legal reasoning and its kinds are things which were invented also in later ages, and no one thinks they are innovations.[3] Such should also be our attitude toward philosophical reasoning. There is another reason why it should be so, but this is not the proper place to mention it. A large number of the followers of this religion confirm philosophical reasoning, all except a small worthless minority, who argue from religious ordinances. Now, as it is established that the Law makes the consideration of philosophical reasoning and its kinds as necessary as legal reasoning, if none of our predecessors has made an effort to enquire into

---

[1]Sharia, or Sacred Law, based on the Quran and Hadith (the traditions of the Prophet and his Companions).

[2]In other words, the Prophet, his Companions, and the early caliphs were ignorant of Aristotelian logic.

[3]Sharia was essential to Islamic life, and legal reasoning was the method employed by Muslim jurists as they attempted to apply the Law to everyday circumstances.

it, we should begin to do it, and so help them, until the knowledge is complete. For if it is difficult or rather impossible for one person to acquaint himself single-handed with all things which it is necessary to know in legal matters, it is still more difficult in the case of philosophical reasoning. And, if before us, somebody has enquired into it, we should derive help from what he has said. It is quite immaterial whether that man is our co-religionist or not; for the instrument by which purification is perfected is not made uncertain in its usefulness by its being in the hands of one of our own party, or of a foreigner, if it possesses the attributes of truth. By these latter we mean those Ancients who investigated these things before the advent of Islam.

Now, such is the case. All that is wanted in an enquiry into philosophical reasoning has already been perfectly examined by the Ancients. All that is required of us is that we should go back to their books and see what they have said in this connection. If all that they say be true, we should accept it and if there be something wrong, we should be warned by it. Thus, when we have finished this kind of research we shall have acquired instruments by which we can observe the universe, and consider its general character. For so long as one does not know its general character one cannot know the created, and so long as he does not know the created, he can have no knowledge of the Creator. Thus, we must begin an enquiry into the universe systematically.

Averröes, *The Philosophy and Theology of Averroes,* trans. Mohammed Jamil-al-Rahman (Baroda: A. G. Widgery, 1921), 14–20.

■ Roger Bacon on Experiment

The greatest proponent of experimentation of the medieval Latin West was the thirteenth-century English Franciscan friar and university professor Roger Bacon (died ca. 1292). Bacon believed that the science of his time was excessively theoretical and dependent on logic, and advocated a reform that would place more emphasis on experience. This did not mean a rejection of Aristotle. Bacon, an admirer of Aristotle, claimed that true understanding of his works would lead to a more empirical science. The following extract from Bacon's *Opus Maius (Greater Work)* sets forth an experimental program.

How does Bacon describe "experience"? Why is it so important? Is experience sufficient of and by itself, according to Bacon? Why or why not? According to Bacon, where does experience stand in relation to Divine Revelation? What would Bacon say regarding those who maintain there can be no accommodation between science and religion? How does he analyze the weaknesses of Latin science in his own time? It has been written of Roger Bacon that he was "one of the earliest advocates of the modern scientific method." In the light of what you read here, does this seem an accurate evaluation of the man and his approach to science?

———————————————

Having laid down the main points of the wisdom of the Latins as regards language, mathematics and optics, I wish now to review the principles of wisdom from the point of view of experimental science, because without experiment it is impossible to know anything thoroughly.

There are two ways of acquiring knowledge, one through reason, the other by experiment. Argument reaches a conclusion and compels us to admit it, but it neither makes us certain nor so annihilates doubt that the mind rests calm in the intuition of truth, unless it finds this certitude by way of experience. Thus, many have arguments toward attainable facts, but because they have not experienced them, they overlook them and neither avoid a harmful nor follow a beneficial course. Even if a man that has never seen fire, proves by good reasoning that fire burns, and devours and destroys things, nevertheless the mind of one hearing his arguments would never be convinced, nor would he avoid fire until he puts his hand or some combustible thing into it in order to prove by experiment what the argument taught. But after the fact of combustion is experienced, the mind is satisfied and lies calm in the certainty of truth. Hence argument is not enough, but experience is.

This is evident even in mathematics, where demonstration is the surest. The mind of a man that receives that clearest of demonstrations concerning the equilateral triangle without experiment will never stick to the conclusion nor act upon it till confirmed by experiment by means of the intersection of two circles from either section of which two lines are drawn to the ends of a given line. Then one receives the conclusion without doubt. What Aristotle says of the demonstration by the syllogism being able to give knowledge, can be understood if it is accompanied by experience, but not of the bare demonstration. What he says in the first book of the *Metaphysics*, that those knowing the reason and cause are wiser than the experienced, he speaks concerning the experienced who know the bare fact only without the cause. But I speak here of the experienced that know the reason and cause through their experience. And such are perfect in their knowledge, as Aristotle wishes to be in the sixth book of the *Ethics*, whose simple statements are to be believed as if they carried demonstration, as he says in that very place.

Whoever wishes without proof to revel in the truths of things need only know how to neglect experience. This is evident from examples. Authors write many things and the people cling to them through arguments which they make without experiment, that are utterly false. It is commonly believed among all classes that one can break adamant[4] only with the blood of a goat, and philosophers and theologians strengthen this myth. But it is not yet proved by adamant being broken by blood of this kind, as much as it is argued to this conclusion. And yet, even without the blood it can be broken with ease. I have seen this with my eyes; and this must needs be because gems cannot be cut out save by the breaking of the stone. Similarly it is commonly believed that the secretions of the beaver that the doctors use are the testicles of the male, but this is not so, as the beaver has this secretion beneath its breast and even the male as well as the female produces a secretion of this kind. In addition also to this secretion, the male has its testicles in the natural place and thus again it is a horrible lie that, since hunters chase the beaver for this secretion, the beaver knowing what they are after, tears out his testicles with his teeth and throws them away. Again it is popularly said that cold water in a vase freezes more quickly than hot; and the argument for this is that contrary is excited by the contrary, like enemies running together. They even impute this to Aristotle in the second book of *Meteorology*,[5] but he certainly did not say this, but says something like it by which they have been deceived, that if both cold and hot water are poured into a cold place as on ice, the cold freezes quicker (which is true), but if they are placed in two vases, the hot will freeze quicker. It is necessary, then, to prove everything by experience.

Experience is of two kinds. One is through the external senses: such are the experiments that are made upon the heavens through instruments in regard to facts there, and the facts on Earth that we prove in various ways to be certain in our own sight. And facts that are not true in places where we are, we know through other wise men that have experienced them. Thus, Aristotle with the authority of Alexander, sent 2,000 men throughout various parts of the Earth in order to learn at first hand everything on the surface of the world, as Pliny says in his *Natural History*.[6] And this experience is human and philosophical just as far as a man is able to make use of the beneficent grace given to him, but such experience is not enough for man, because it does not give full certainty as regards corporeal things because of their complexity and touches the spiritual not at all. Hence man's intellect must be aided in another way, and thus the patriarchs and prophets[7] who first gave

---

[4]A diamond.

[5]In his *Meteorologica*, Aristotle dealt with all Earth sciences, not just the weather.

[6]Pliny the Elder (died 79 CE), Roman natural scientist and encyclopedist.

[7]Of the Tanakh or Jewish Bible, known to Christians as the Old Testament.

science to the world secured inner light and did not rest entirely on the senses. So also many of the faithful since Christ. For grace makes many things clear to the faithful, and there is divine inspiration not alone concerning spiritual but even about corporeal things. In accordance with which Ptolemy says in the *Centilogium*[8] that there is a double way of coming to the knowledge of things, one through the experiments of science, the other through divine inspiration, which latter is far the better as he says.

_____

Roger Bacon, "On Experimental Science" ed. Oliver Joseph Thatcher, *The Library of Original Sources* (Milwaukee: University Research Extension, 1915), 369–371.

■ A Jewish Physician and Christian Medicine: Prologue to Leon Joseph of Carcassonne's Hebrew Translation of Gerard de Solo's *Practica super nono Almansoris*

By the thirteenth and fourteenth centuries, Jewish physicians in the Mediterranean were becoming more interested in the Scholastic science and medicine of European universities. Since Jews were forbidden to enter Christian universities, it was necessary to translate Latin works into Hebrew to make them available to Jewish doctors. At the end of the fourteenth century or in the early fifteenth century, Leon Joseph of Carcassonne, a physician who once resided in this city of southern France (until the Jews were expelled from it in 1394), translated a Latin commentary on the ninth book of the Al-Mansur, a medical encyclopedia compiled by the Persian physician al-Razi known to the West as Rhazes.

What were the barriers to disseminating this knowledge in the Jewish community that Leon Joseph saw? How did he overcome these barriers? What were his motivations for making this translation? Compare the views of Ibn Rushd, Roger Bacon, and Leon Joseph on two issues: 1) How did each perceive the relationship of science (or philosophy) to religion in his own day? Were they comfortably accommodating one another or not? 2) What did each think was the proper relationship of rational inquiry to religion? What conclusions follow from this comparative analysis?

_____

[8]The *Centilogium*, or *One Hundred Words*, is a collection of 100 sentences ascribed to Ptolemy.

Thus, says Leon Joseph, the translator, who lives in Carcassonne. Many years ago I directed my attention toward the study of and research into the profane sciences, which are several in number and nature; in number they are as many as the days of the week, and each one has its own subject matter. I had placed my confidence in them in order to undertake various pieces of research. In my eyes, the merits of these sciences were above all praise. This explains my zeal and wish to know them and master them. I, therefore, followed in the footsteps of the learned men of our own times, as well as those of the distant and recent past who have had such concerns, so that they should illuminate my way with the light of their intelligence and understanding; I said to myself that they must have achieved the level that had been acquired by those perfect men long since disappeared.

But I realized that the lack of knowledge that they, and some of my people at this time, found themselves submerged in was great and immense, and their words concerning the profane[9] sciences were like "the words of a sealed book."[10] Thus I said unto myself: perhaps my wish is greater than my intelligence, and the defect is mine for not being able to fathom the concepts, and it is my own lack of intelligence, the weakness of my spirit and my ignorance, that to not allow me to understand their words, and not their ignorance and their lack of knowledge, for they are the most learned among all men and I am nothing but the lowest of their class. . . . I perceived that the lack of knowledge among one sector of our nation was by no means strange. . . .

Then I heard a voice telling me that there was not one single cause, but many, for the lack and absence of this knowledge among many of our scholars. Sciences defeated them because their subject matter is more rational than in the bosom of our people, and they are as far from them as east is from west, and all the more so from the fundamentals of the Torah[11] and of religious faith.

For this reason, some of our scholars refrained from studying them, from learning about them, and from investigating their aims; but others among them, who by the mercy of God studied them with the intention of selecting what was fit to eat from what was only fit for throwing away . . . decided to do so in secret and unknown to others. And all this they did for fear of the tongues of the foolish among the people. . . . And also for fear of those learned in the Torah, who proscribed the superfluous

---

[9]Secular, or nonsacred. Theology is a sacred science.

[10]Isaiah 29:11, in which the prophet states that for the Jews, every prophecy and vision from God is like the words in a sealed book.

[11]The Law, namely the first five books of the Hebrew Bible, or Tanakh.

from our souls; whose power over wise men comes not from strength nor from the breadth of their knowledge, but rather from the strength of their hands and from their many ruses that make the mass of the common people believe whatever they think, that is to say, that these sciences and those who possess them are sundered from the community of those that possess the Torah.

Another problem for Jews wishing to become physicians and scientists is bad translations.

When I realized all this, I said to myself; there are no learned and expert men in our region. And I went in search of wise Christians so that they should guide me in such matters and so that they should show me the way, and so that they should show me old and new volumes. Among them I saw the works of the learned physician Gordon,[12] who was outstanding on the majority of subjects, both in theoretical study and in practical matters, and who achieved great fame. . . . The Jews who translated in this land gained access to it by means of the vernacular, they expressed the Latin in Romance,[13] adding that not every Latin word may be translated into the vernacular tongue, and then they expressed it in the sacred language.[14] . . . Seeking among their books, I found two new books, "two golden pipes,"[15] exemplary, excellent and worthy, which the people of our nation do not know. They are the books by the learned Gerard de Solo and by the master Jean de Tournemire,[16] of whose existence I had known for ten years, but which I had been unable to acquire, neither in Montpellier,[17] even though it was their place of origin, nor in Avignon,[18] nor in other important places, since there were but very few copies and since the learned men of Montpellier anathematize and excommunicate anybody who should sell to those who are not Christians. In order to acquire them, I invested all the funds that I was able, without reflecting on the consequences. . . . The truth is I paid double the price for them, owing to the yearning and

---

[12]Bernard de Gourdon, a professor of medicine at Montpellier from about 1283 to sometime before 1330.

[13]That is they translated it into Provençal, the Romance language of Languedoc (present-day southern France).

[14]Hebrew.

[15]Two golden, or valuable, manuscripts.

[16]Gerard de Solo, who flourished in the early fourteenth century, was a physician, professor, and rector at the University of Montpellier, which had the most prestigious medical faculty north of the Alps. Jean de Tournemire, who flourished in the last half of the fourteenth century, possibly dying around 1396, was also a physician and professor at Montpellier. See note 18.

[17]See note 16.

[18]Where the Roman papacy then resided. Jean de Tournemire served as a papal physician at Avignon.

desire that I felt for them. I saw their excellence, and that they explained things and answered matters in a suitable way. He who acts with them is as if he were grasping a column; he will fear nothing, not even ten thousand physicians who might come with proofs and disputes, for they are pure flour. . . .

Behold, thus, that I begin the book of Gerard, based on book nine of the *Book of Almansor* [by al-Razi] short in length but great in quality, stronger than a rock. . . . When God wishes I should finish it, I shall undertake Tournemire's book; in his time he was head of all the scholars of Montpellier, who were placed beneath him. I saw him with my own eyes and I spoke with him. He was a man who was pleasant to talk to. His behavior was not like that of the other scholars of his generation, who scorned those Jews who practiced the art of medicine for he guided them as much as he was able. May his soul rest in the treasure where the souls of the pious among gentile people live! . . .

I took the decision to translate these books, not for myself, but for the people of my nation, both those who live alongside me today and those who will come after, and who do not know the language of the Christians at all. When they examine it and read it, they will see the perfection, the beauty, and the order of these books, they will bless me because of them and they will remember me for having been the reason why they should find them and the reason why they are able to compare themselves with the physicians in proofs and arguments, and this is a second life.

From Luis Garcia-Ballester, Lola Ferre, and Eduard Feliu, "Jewish Appreciation of Fourteenth-Century Scholastic Medicine," *Osiris* second series, vol. 6 (University of Chicago Press, 1990), 106–114.

The Jesuits and World Science, 1540–1773

Modern science is full of organizations, from disciplinary organizations like the American Physics Association to elite interdisciplinary groups like Britain's Royal Society. But the first organization to gather, publish, and circulate scientific information worldwide was not an association of scientists, but the Society of Jesus, a Roman Catholic religious order. This may come as a surprise. When many of us think of the history of the Catholic Church and science, particularly in the early modern period, the first thing that comes to mind is the trial of Galileo Galilei (1564–1642) for publicly arguing that the Earth revolves around the Sun. Galileo was tried by the Inquisition, and ultimately forced to recant his position. No wonder that we often think of the church as an opponent of science. However, the story of the Jesuits from their founding in 1540 to their (temporary) suppression by papal order in 1773 shows that reality is more complex than that.

The Jesuits, founded by a Spanish-Basque soldier-turned-priest, Ignatius Loyola (1495–1556), and his small band of followers, were officially recognized by Pope Paul III (Pope 1534–1549) in 1540, at a time when the Catholic Church faced two great challenges. One was from Protestants, who in the previous decades had broken away from the authority of Rome in vast areas of Europe, including England, Scandinavia, and a large part of Germany. The other was from the enormous populations of non-Christians in Asia and the Americas that Spanish and Portuguese explorations and conquests had opened up for missionary activity. In this challenging and exciting era for Catholicism, the Jesuits grew rapidly. They numbered a thousand in Loyola's own time and 8,500 by the end of the century.

Following a strategy of conversion from the top down, the Jesuits appealed to intellectual elites, but Loyola and his first companions were not particularly interested in science. Nevertheless, the Jesuits found themselves pulled into science in two ways.

One was their involvement in education. All Jesuits were required to have university educations, and they saw the excellence of their own schools as a weapon with which to combat Protestantism. By 1750, the height of the Society of Jesus before its suppression, the Jesuits operated over 500 educational establishments in Europe and about another hundred overseas.

Although Latin and Greek formed the heart of their official plan of studies (*ratio atque institutio studiorum*), which they laid out in 1599, natural philosophy and mathematics were important parts of the Jesuit curriculum. The Jesuits needed professors in these disciplines, and they rapidly emerged as the scientific elite among Catholic religious orders. A Jesuit professor, Christoph Clavius (1537–1612), was in charge of astronomical consultations to the pope. It was Clavius's work that eventually led to the creation of the Gregorian calendar still used today and named after Pope Gregory XIII (reign 1572–1585), a great supporter of the Jesuits, who initiated action to fulfill the long-standing need for a more accurate calendar.[1] Mathematics was tied to ballistics and fortification, topics of interest to the many aristocratic students in Jesuit schools who planned on military careers. Even Protestant schools used Jesuit books, such as Clavius's excellent mathematical textbooks.

---

[1] Despite the superiority of the Gregorian calendar, its Catholic provenance proved a stumbling block for many Protestants. The Protestant states of the Holy Roman Empire and Denmark did not adopt the Gregorian calendar until 1699, Great Britain until 1752, and Sweden until 1753.

CHRISTOPHORVS CLAVIVS BAMBERGENSIS E
SOCIETATE IESV ÆTATIS SVÆ ANNO LXIX
Franciscus Villamœna Fe Rome Anno 1606 Cum privilegio Summi Pontificis et Superiorum authoritate.

Christoph Clavius (1537–1612). *New York Public Library*

Jesuits were also drawn into science through missionary work. The sixteenth and seventeenth centuries saw a great wave of Catholic missionary effort, while Protestants did not begin to rival Catholics as overseas missionaries until the nineteenth century. Catholic missionaries reached territories newly subject to European empires, especially Spanish and Portuguese America, where they drew on the support of imperial and royal authorities. They also reached societies totally independent of any European domination, ranging from the great empires of China and Mughal India to the Native American peoples of Canada and the present-day American Midwest, where they were on their own.

As the cutting edge of a revived Roman Church, the Jesuits were leaders in this Catholic missionary effort. One of the earliest Jesuits, Jerome Nadal (1507–1580), had proposed the motto *Totus mundus nostra habitatio fit*—"the whole world is our dwelling place." The Jesuits were represented in every inhabited continent except Australia, which Europeans only learned about in the eighteenth century. By 1750, the Jesuits had around 270 mission stations scattered over the globe. As missionary-scholars, they both taught Western science and gathered information for European scientists. Their worldwide reach was unparalleled until scientific societies spread across Europe and its colonies in the eighteenth century. The global dispersal of the Jesuit order gave it a unique ability to gather observations in geoscience and astronomy from different vantage points. In one of the first efforts at global coordination of data gathering, the French priest and astronomer Marin Mersenne (1588–1648), a member of the rival Minim Order, urged the Jesuits to make coordinated observations of lunar eclipses and magnetic variation. He recognized that only the Jesuits combined a global presence with the necessary training. The importance of the missionary effort also influenced Jesuit teaching in Europe, insofar as navigation and cartography became important parts of the curriculum at many Jesuit institutions.

Early modern Jesuits produced over 4,000 books and 600 journal articles dealing with science, as well as over a thousand unprinted manuscripts, far exceeding the output of any other Catholic religious order. Jesuit scientists included Niccolo Cabeo (1586–1650), one of the earliest explorers of magnetism, and the lunar cartographer Giambattista Riccioli (1598–1671).

Jesuits were also among the most mobile of early modern European scientists, not just over the world but within Europe. A cosmopolitan community, which paid little regard to the national or class origin of its members, the Jesuits were ideally positioned to circulate scientific ideas and to advance bright young men of humble background to positions of influence. Advancement within the society was one of the most meritocratic systems in early modern Europe.

This flexibility was a double-edged sword as far as Jesuit science was concerned. Jesuits were less rooted in a particular discipline than other early modern scientists because it was the usual practice of Jesuit schools to rotate professors through the disciplines. (There were, however, some exceptions such as Clavius.) While the rotation might lead to an enviable breadth, it often worked against deep knowledge of a particular discipline. What is more, their unwavering devotion to the Roman Catholic Church and its doctrines also compromised the Jesuits' work as scientists.

JESUIT SCIENCE AND RELIGION

The sixteenth and seventeenth centuries were the time of the European "Scientific Revolution," a series of changes in both the content and practice of natural philosophy that led directly to modern science. One of the major intellectual struggles was between the Copernican theory of astronomy, which stated that the Sun is motionless and orbited by the Earth and planets, and the older theory that placed the Earth at the center of the universe. A second, linked struggle was between traditional Aristotelian physics, which depended on the Earth's central position, and the new, Copernicanism-compatible "mechanical philosophies," which emerged in the early seventeenth century. The Jesuits, like the Catholic Church as an institution, supported traditional natural philosophy and opposed the new theories.

Jesuits were required not just to defend Catholic doctrine in matters scientific (as in all other areas) but to believe it. Loyola had specifically required Jesuits to believe that white was black, if that was the church's decree, so believing that the Sun went around the Earth was not much of a challenge to a good Jesuit. Jesuits, such as the astronomer and sunspot expert Christopher Scheiner (1573–1650), led the opposition to Galileo's Copernicanism. Although there was some intellectual pluralism among the early Jesuits, in 1611 the General of the Order, Claudio Aquaviva (1543–1615), decreed that Jesuits were required to defend the authority of Aristotle in philosophy. As a result, in the seventeenth and eighteenth centuries, Jesuits fell increasingly behind other European scientists, Protestant and Catholic, who were free to reject Aristotle's authority. Moreover, Jesuits avoided potentially dangerous theoretical commitments by not broadening their individual discoveries into general arguments on natural philosophy and were often willing to put forth and analyze a number of explanations for phenomena without necessarily picking one out as the truth.

The Jesuits subordinated natural philosophy to religious ends in other ways, as well. Knowledge of the true God was essential for a correct understanding of God's creation. The first great Jesuit missionary to Asia, Francis Xavier (1506–1552), saw supposed Japanese backwardness in science as a consequence of their lack of belief in a creator. If they did not understand a creator, how could they understand creation? Much Jesuit scientific work was dedicated to searching for the signs and emblems of God everywhere in the created universe. Athanasius Kircher (1601–1680), the leading Jesuit scientist and collector of antiquities and other curiosities in the middle of the seventeenth century, was as fascinated by stones formed in the shape of the cross or of various religious symbols and personalities as he was by the properties of magnets.

THE JESUITS AS SCIENTIFIC MISSIONARIES IN CHINA

Science played a central role in the Jesuit missionary effort in China. Christianity could not be imposed by force upon the vast, vigorous, and wealthy Chinese Empire. Instead missionaries had to find ways to make Christianity appealing to the Chinese. The Italian Jesuit Matteo Ricci (1552–1610) devised a missionary strategy of "conversion from the top," a strategy that was widely practiced by Jesuits in non-Western societies but was controversial within the Catholic Church. Jesuits hoped that by converting Chinese courtiers, officials, and intellectuals to Christianity, they could create protectors for missionaries working in the field and their Christian communities. The disastrous failure of the Catholic mission to Japan, where the government had expelled missionaries and suppressed Christianity, was on everyone's mind. Ultimately, Jesuits hoped to convert the emperor, who would make China an officially Christian country. Change at the top would open the door for missionaries to convert the masses of people, and eventually, along with Chinese Christians, set up an institutional Catholic Church in the country. This model of conversion drew on the historical (and recent) experience of Christianity in Europe, where the conversion of a ruler usually led to the conversion of a region or country. It required Jesuits like Ricci to adopt the manner of life and learn the complex culture of the Chinese intellectual elite.

Ricci's plan depended on the Jesuits' making themselves sufficiently interesting and valuable to the Chinese scholarly and political class that they would be able to persuade them to accept Christianity. Science was one of the society's principal assets in this endeavor. Not all Western science was potentially useful for the missionaries, however. The publication of works of Aristotelian natural philosophy and Galenic medicine in Chinese had little effect on their intended audiences—the Chinese had their own systems of natural philosophy and medicine to which Western systems were not obviously superior. But in astronomy the Jesuits and their Chinese pupils had several advantages over traditional Chinese scientists, despite the Jesuit rejection of Copernicanism. These advantages included better instruments and mathematics and a more accurate cosmology based on a spherical Earth, while some traditional Chinese thinking identified the Earth as flat. Other areas of Western superiority that Ricci and his successors exploited were geographical knowledge, cartography, and clock making.

China had a long history of state involvement in science. Areas of government concern included disciplines with obvious practical applications, including medicine, agronomy, and geography. Astronomy was important for calendrical reasons. The Chinese calendar was "lunisolar," combining a lunar month with a solar year. Since lunar months don't go evenly into solar years, lunisolar calendars require frequent adjustments. The production of an accurate calendar that also set forth the dates, times, and durations of eclipses and other celestial phenomena was an important testimony to the emperor's possession of the "Mandate of Heaven," the source of legitimacy in traditional Chinese political theory. Unpredicted or wrongly predicted eclipses were bad omens for the ruling dynasty. Such was the close connection between astronomy and politics that private ownership or use of astronomical equipment was forbidden.

The Astronomical Board, which had the responsibility for creating the calendar, had institutional roots as far back as the Han dynasty (206 BCE–220 CE). Such was the importance of a good calendar that the Board had a long tradition of hiring foreign astronomers from India and Islamic lands to supplement traditional Chinese reckoning. Indian astronomers and astrologers had come to China, along with Buddhism, in the third century CE. China's incorporation into the vast Mongol Empire during the Yuan dynasty (1279–1368) had led to increased interaction with the Islamic world, and the Astronomical Board of the Ming (1368–1644) had a section staffed by Muslim astronomers employing Islamic methods and instruments. The idea of employing foreigners to help make the calendar was not new to the

Chinese, but the Jesuits were far more successful than any preceding group of foreign astronomers.

The calendrical situation became particularly acute in 1592, when the Board missed the time of a lunar eclipse by a day. Ricci was not a trained astronomer, but he had been a student of Clavius. He would have learned geometry, trigonometry, cosmological theory, and the use of basic astronomical instruments at the Collegio Romano, the Jesuit college in Rome. In 1605, he wrote to Rome imploring his superiors to send trained astronomers, but until they arrived (after Ricci's death in 1610), he was able to impress the Chinese by predicting eclipses and adjusting sundials.

Building on Ricci's early success, some early seventeenth-century missionaries published astronomical works in Chinese, setting forth Western cosmological schemes and even reporting Galileo's telescopic discoveries. Along with astronomy, they introduced elements of Western mathematics, such as trigonometry and logarithms. Ricci's posthumously published Chinese textbook of arithmetic, *Translations of Guidelines for Practical Arithmetic* (1614), blended Clavius's popular *Epitome of Practical Arithmetic* with Chinese elements. A telescope was ceremonially presented to the emperor in 1634. The Catholic Church's condemnation of Copernicanism in 1616, however, meant that the missionaries' version of European science increasingly diverged from that of Europe itself, where Copernicanism was becoming the dominant theory in Protestant countries and France. Like the Jesuits in Europe, during the 1630s missionaries in China compromised with Copernicanism by shifting their cosmology from the Ptolemaic system to the Danish astronomer Tycho Brahe's (1546–1601) picture of a stationary Earth with the Sun and moon rotating around it and the planets around the Sun. The Tychonic system, mathematically equivalent to the Copernican, had some of Copernicanism's elegance and ease of calculation while avoiding the physical and religious problems caused by a moving Earth. Heliocentric Copernicanism would not be introduced to the Chinese until the mid-eighteenth century, when the French Jesuit Michel Benoist (1715–1774) explained the system in a document submitted to the Chinese court, although without endorsing its truth.

Ricci and his immediate successors did, indeed, win some prominent converts among the elite through first interesting them in Western science. Li Zhizao (1565–1630), a Confucian official and early convert who became known as one of the "Three pillars of

Christianity in China," was initially attracted to Ricci's world map, which presented a two-dimensional projection of a three-dimensional, round Earth. Convinced by the Westerners' claims that the traditional Chinese idea of the flat Earth was wrong, Li studied further in both Western geography and cartography and in Christianity, which he treated together in a book he published under the title *Learning from Heaven* (1628).

THE JESUITS AS IMPERIAL ASTRONOMERS AND CARTOGRAPHERS

Over the course of the seventeenth century, Ricci's program of appealing to the Chinese intellectual elite—the Confucian literati—was increasingly eclipsed by a close alliance with the Chinese state. One reason for this was the overthrow of the Ming dynasty and its replacement by the Qing dynasty in the 1644. The Qing were an alien dynasty—the leaders of the non-Chinese Manchu people from the area northeast of China who invaded and conquered the country. Johann Adam Schall von Bell's (1591–1666) successful prediction led the powerful Manchu Prince-Regent Dorgon to offer him the position of head of the Astronomical Board. He accepted, setting a precedent that would be followed by European Jesuits until news of the suppression of the order reached China in 1774. The politically sure-footed Schall[2] quickly replaced astronomers trained in Islamic and traditional Chinese methods with experts in Western astronomy. Since Jesuits were sworn to the vow of poverty, the salaries paid to Jesuits at the Astronomical Board were handed over to the Jesuit China mission, and were important in its financing. Schall von Bell's most important successor, the Belgian Jesuit Ferdinand Verbiest (1623–1688), would oversee the final defeat of the old guard in the bureau and become the mathematical tutor and astronomical instrument-maker to the longest-reigning and most scholarly of the Qing rulers, the Kangxi Emperor (reign 1661–1722).

Jesuit astronomy was controversial within the Catholic Church. The great rivals of the Jesuits were the mendicant friars, or "begging brothers"—the Franciscans and Dominicans. The mendicants believed

---

[2]Schall von Bell even appealed to the emperor on the grounds that both Europeans and Manchus were foreigners in China.

that the best way to convert non-Christian societies was to start by preaching to the poor, following the example of the apostles. They saw the Jesuits as too intimate with the non-Christian Chinese elite. Mendicants pointed out that the Chinese calendar was intimately associated with traditional Chinese culture, much of which was "idolatrous." The function of the calendar in designating lucky and unlucky days, for example, had no Christian justification, and Jesuit involvement in Chinese calendar-making was a betrayal of Christianity.

Another area where Qing emperors found Western Jesuits useful was cartography. The Qing were one of the great expansionist dynasties in Chinese history, taking Taiwan from the Dutch and extending Chinese power deep into Tibet and Central Asia. Like other empires, they wanted accurate maps of the new territories they controlled. In addition to drawing from Arabic mapmakers, China had its own cartographic tradition, which had reached a peak of excellence in the Middle Ages and had exceeded the productions of then contemporary European mapmakers. However, European expansion in the early modern period had led to a refinement of cartographical techniques, including the creation of a standard system of latitude and longitude. By the seventeenth century, European surveying and cartographical skills exceeded China's. The Kangxi Emperor was particularly interested in cartography, and he collaborated in this technical science with a particular set of Jesuits from France. While the early Jesuits of Ricci's generation had used science only as one of several means to reach the Chinese elite, science lay at the heart of the French Jesuit mission. The French Jesuits arrived in China as part of the effort by Louis XIV's (reign 1643–1715) France, already Europe's dominant power, to dislodge the hold that Portugal, through the archbishopric of Goa, had on the Catholic Church in South and East Asia. The French Jesuits, who explicitly identified themselves as technical experts rather than missionaries, had been chosen for their mathematical and cartographic abilities and represented the French state rather than the Catholic Church.

Combining Chinese geographical knowledge, their own explorations, and European cartographic techniques, the Jesuits helped produce the best map of the Chinese Empire to that date, first published in 1717. The Jesuits were only part of a massive, state-organized effort to produce the map, but an important one. The survey was followed by another between 1756 and 1759. However, the overall Jesuit project of converting the empire to Christianity was making little progress, even though Jesuit writings claimed the missionary fathers used the opportunity presented by the survey of the empire to preach Christianity in its remote regions.

THE CHINESE AND JESUIT SCIENCE

The Jesuit scientific mission would not have been as successful as it was if the Chinese intelligentsia had not been ready for it. The corruption and inefficiency of late Ming government caused many Chinese scholars to question the Neo-Confucian orthodoxy that dominated the government civil-service examinations. Both the metaphysics of the dominant, "official" Neo-Confucian School founded by the Song dynasty scholar Zhu Xi (1130–1200) and the psychological subjectivity of its main rival, the school of Wang Yangming (1472–1529), were challenged in the name of a more philosophically materialistic and empirical Confucianism. The search for new knowledge made some Chinese intellectuals listen to the Jesuits, particularly as the missionaries were careful to present their scientific and religious ideas as compatible with a "true" Confucianism rooted in the ancient classics rather than later Neo-Confucian interpretations.

Both the empirical and theoretical aspects of Jesuit science interested the Chinese literati. The detailed maps of Europe and much of the Americas that the Jesuits brought greatly added to the store of Chinese geographical information. Moreover, inasmuch as traditional Chinese astronomy was centered on prediction, and not explanation, China had not developed an elaborate cosmological theory on how the Sun, moon, stars, planets, and Earth interacted. The Jesuits now seemed to provide one readymade. Indeed, Jesuit writings led to greater concern among Chinese astronomers for physical descriptions of the cosmos as opposed to algebraic techniques for predicting planetary movements. One astronomer, Wang Xichan (1628–1682), probably never met a Westerner, but learned the Tychonic system and techniques such as trigonometry from Jesuit astronomical manuals. He used this knowledge to introduce, for the first time in China, methods of predicting solar transits and planetary occultations (occasions when one celestial body appears to move in front of another, relative to an observer on Earth). He also invented a new cosmology based on Tycho's system, with substantial modifications.

Some scholars viewed the new knowledge as a threat. There was a brief crackdown on the Jesuits led by a Confucian Chinese official named Shen Que. Shen Que submitted a memorial (official memorandum) to the emperor in 1616 summarizing the ways in which the Jesuits presented a threat to the traditional Chinese order. The challenge posed by the Westerners' new astronomical ideas figured prominently among them. Despite the fears of officials like Shen Que, Western astronomy never displaced or even seriously rivaled the prestige of the native tradition. To legitimate the study of Jesuit astronomy by the Chinese, late seventeenth-century Chinese scholars such as Mei Wending argued that "Western" science was originally Chinese knowledge that had traveled westward due to the many wars of early Chinese history. It had been forgotten in its native land, but developed in the barbarian kingdoms of the West. Now, it had returned to China. Asserting that foreign ideas were originally Chinese was a common Chinese method of assimilating them. A common pattern of astronomical training in eighteenth-century China was to study Western writings, and then progress to the Chinese astronomical classics. Jesuit-introduced methods of astronomical computation could be grafted onto the body of Chinese astronomical thought, as Indian and Islamic methods had been earlier. Ultimately, the greatest impact of Western astronomy on China was the revitalization of the indigenous Chinese astronomical tradition.

The Kangxi Emperor and other early Qing rulers made a conscious attempt to draw the sciences, which had been largely intellectually independent in earlier dynasties, into the orbit of classical Confucian scholarship. Incorporating the parts of Western science that the Qing wanted to use into a basically Chinese-centered narrative was part of this process. The Kangxi Emperor had a particular interest in mathematics, in which he had been tutored by Jesuits early in his reign. He ordered the translation of Euclid's geometry textbook from a Chinese version into Manchu, the language of China's rulers, and in 1713 commissioned a group of Chinese scholars to compile a mathematical survey. The survey was largely based on Jesuit works but presented its mathematics as based on ancient Chinese learning. The Kangxi Emperor was interested in Western medicine, particularly after Jesuits had successfully treated him with their new discovery, quinine. He also sponsored the publication of a Western anatomical treatise in Manchu. However, only a few copies were printed, and the fact that Western anatomical knowledge was not widely available in Chinese—the written language of the vast majority of physicians and scholars in the empire—meant that the work of the Jesuit anatomists had little impact on Chinese medical thought.

Jesuit science also had effects beyond China. Other societies of East Asia—Korea, Japan, and to a lesser extent Vietnam—looked to China as a cultural leader. The intellectuals of these countries were as familiar with written Chinese as the intellectuals of Europe were familiar with Latin and Greek. Consequently, Chinese-Jesuit books made their way to Korea and Japan, where they were read by scholars.

THE DECLINE OF JESUIT SCIENCE IN CHINA

The decline of Jesuit science in China during the eighteenth century stemmed from Jesuit science's increasing backwardness as compared to European science and from a cultural turning-inward characteristic of the mid-Qing period. Catholic astronomers and physicists in the late seventeenth and eighteenth-century faced the problem that Western astronomy was increasingly Copernican and its physics increasingly Newtonian. The Jesuits in China, who were not just religiously but geographically isolated from the mainstream of European science, were falling increasingly far behind. In 1683, Verbiest presented the Kangxi Emperor with a massive compilation of Aristotelian commentary in Chinese, *Studies to Exhaustively Master Principles (Qiongli xue)* at a time when Aristotelian physics in Europe was moribund and Isaac Newton's *Mechanical Principles of Natural Philosophy*, the foundation of eighteenth-century physics, was just four years away from publication.

The Jesuits' role as imperial officials also proved a liability, as they lost their broader connections with the Chinese Confucian intelligentsia, particularly those who lived outside Beijing, to which the Jesuits were largely confined. However, changes in Confucianism itself also diminished contacts between Jesuits and Chinese scholars outside the court. The most important Confucian movement of the eighteenth century, *kaozheng* or "evidential-research" scholarship, presented itself as a return to the original meaning of Confucius. *Kaozheng* scholars meticulously studied the ancient Chinese past, rejecting foreign knowledge, as well as the Neo-Confucian innovations of the Song and Ming dynasties, to return to an idealized version of Han dynasty scholarship. Although there was some Jesuit influence at the origin of the *kaozheng* tradition, Jesuit science was of little interest to *kaozheng* scholars in and of itself, only in the light it might throw on the Confucian classics.

The larger failure of the Jesuit mission in China was that it could not convince the Chinese that Western knowledge comprised a unity, in which the excellence of Western science and mathematics was testimony to the superiority of Western religion. The Confucian literati and imperial bureaucracy continued to view science and religion as separate fields. The usefulness of Western astronomy and mathematics no more convinced them to adopt Christianity than the usefulness of Islamic astronomy had convinced their predecessors to adopt Islam.

In brief, Jesuits played a role as technical experts but could not change Chinese culture. Eighteenth-century Jesuits helped design and build the Summer Palace of the Qianlong Emperor (reign 1736–1795), but their scientific and technical knowledge could not build a Christian China.

JESUIT SCIENCE IN SPANISH AMERICA

The role of science in the Jesuit missions of South and Central America was quite different from the one it played in China. The Jesuits in Latin America did not have the respect for the indigenous peoples of the Americas that Ricci and his successors had for the powerful and independent empire of China with its advanced technology and long tradition of learning. Missionaries in the Spanish and Portuguese American Empires were representatives of a conquering power that hoped to convert indigenous people through the forcible suppression of their previous religion coupled with preaching, not by dazzling them with the glories of European science.

Science was, however, important to the Jesuit mission. Jesuits in Spanish America, like missionaries from other orders, were primarily collectors and analysts rather than disseminators of knowledge, and their science was part of the Spanish (and Catholic) imperial project. The Spanish government, from shortly after the conquest of Mexico and Peru in the early sixteenth century, was concerned to exploit the resources of the conquered countries. In order to efficiently rule these new territories, it needed to know their resources. Jesuits—men trained in science, who were willing to go long distances and stay in remote locations for decades—were ideal for the purpose of "taking inventory" of the new possessions. The Jesuits became even more closely identified with the Spanish Empire with their appointment as its official cosmographers in 1628.

Along with geography and cartography, natural history—the study of the plants, animals, and minerals of a region—played the largest role in early colonial science. The discovery of the Americas was also the discovery of an enormous range of animals and plants previously unknown to European scientists. Colonial natural history had a strongly pragmatic and empirical focus, oriented to identifying the profitable uses of organisms, particularly medical uses. American natural history was different from natural history as practiced in Europe. Old world plants and animals were commonly approached through a thick layer of texts, dating back to Aristotle and earlier. An old world natural historian was frequently as much a bibliographer as a naturalist, and many old world works of natural history were compilations of texts as much as of observations. Natural history in America was more empirical.

The Jesuit José de Acosta (1540–1600) was the greatest natural historian of Spanish America in the sixteenth century. He arrived in Peru as a missionary in 1572 and left in 1586. Acosta's books on his Peruvian experience, notably *Natural and Moral History of the Indies* (1590), promoted the evangelization of the natives of the Americas. Acosta covered the history, geography, weather, plants, animals, and native inhabitants of Peru and Mexico, arguing for the capacity of Native Americans to receive Christianity, provided it was presented in a way suitable for their understandings. Acosta argued that God had providentially prepared the Indians for Christian conversion, and that customs that shocked Europeans did not render them less than human or beyond redemption. This argument led him to examine Native American civilization and place it in a hierarchy of civilizational levels. The highest level was occupied by Europeans and other Old World peoples, such as the Chinese and Japanese, who, all agreed, were suitable for conversion. The Peruvian and Mexican Indians were on the second level of civilization, having cities and state organization but lacking philosophy, and in the case of the Peruvians, written language. Despite their inferiority to Europeans and other fully civilized peoples, the Indians were also suitable for conversion.

Unlike many natural historians of the Spanish and Portuguese Empires, Acosta was a natural philosopher and not a physician or pharmacologist who was primarily interested in the medicinal uses of plants or someone who sought to list new plants and animals and their properties. Rather, Acosta wanted to analyze the New World in overarching Aristotelian terms. He defined the tropical area as over-supplied with water, one of the four Aristotelian elements, along with Earth, air and fire, and suggested the highlands were more suited for human habitation. Acosta was not afraid, however, to contradict specific Aristotelian assertions when they conflicted with reality, pointing out that Aristotle's belief that the tropics would be too hot for human beings had been proven wrong by the explorations of the Spaniards. Proclaiming that experience must supersede following ancient texts, even Christian ones, he pointed out scientific errors in St. Augustine, as well as Aristotle. Although Acosta was struck by the strangeness of the flora, fauna, and inhabitants of the New World, he argued that they had ultimately originated in the Old World, and that all were part of the same divine creation. Acosta was the first to suggest that Native Americans had originated in Asia and crossed over to America across a land bridge in the far north.

Like many books on the Indies, Acosta's were written in Spanish rather than Latin. His audience was not primarily Europe's learned, but included middle- and upper-class Spaniards who did not read Latin. His books were quickly translated into Latin, however, as well as several other European languages, and became one of the basic sources of European knowledge of the New World and its peoples into the eighteenth century.

As in China, in the Americas Jesuits exercised their cartographic skills in the service of empire. The Spaniards faced challenges similar to those of the Qing in delimiting the territories they had acquired. Much surveying was done by missionaries, such as the Italian Jesuit Eusebio Francisco Kino (1645–1711). Kino, who helped establish the first Spanish mission in California, traveled thousands of miles over the southwest helping to establish a Spanish presence in what is today the state of Arizona. His most notable geographic accomplishments were proving that Baja California was a peninsula rather than an island and drawing reliable maps of many southwestern areas that were being measured for the first time.

This historical map shows the exploration route taken by Father Eusebio Francisco Kino, who proved that Baja California was a peninsula rather than an island. *Getty Images Inc.–Hulton Archive Photos*

NATURAL HISTORY AND *MATERIA MEDICA*

One important area of Jesuit scientific research was botany. The age of European discovery and exploration radically transformed botany with thousands of new plants being discovered, brought to Europe either alive or dead, and described. Like other early modern European botanists, Jesuits thought of plants primarily in terms of their medical uses. This meant that the practice of Jesuit natural history was a departure from Loyola's original vision. The founder of the Jesuits had forbidden members of the society to practice medicine, but this prohibition lost its force in the decades following Loyola's death.

The branch of medical science that included finding disease treatments in the natural world was known as *materia medica*. The society had a network of pharmacies at its missionary stations, whose managers were particularly interested in new drugs. Information on American *materia medica* was found not only by experiment, but by talking with and observing indigenous peoples. The people of the Americas had had thousands of years to learn the medical uses of the plants in their regions, and most of the work of Jesuit and other European *materia medica* specialists was incorporating the knowledge of other cultures into the European framework rather than discovering new knowledge.

One exception, and the greatest triumph of Jesuit *materia medica* in South America or anywhere else, was the discovery of the bark of the cinchona tree, which proved an effective specific against the dreaded and common disease of malaria.[3] Malaria, literally "bad air," was believed at the time to spread as a miasma from swamps and other wet areas. (Later study established that it is spread by mosquitoes that breed in stagnant water.) Its symptoms include fever, delirium, shaking, and often death. It was particularly interesting to Jesuits, as the area around Rome was known for its malarial swamps. Malaria prostrated a large portion of the Roman citizenry every summer, and killed several cardinals while they were in Rome to elect a pope in 1623. Cinchona bark was not introduced into the Western pharmacopeia as a remedy for malaria the way most new world drugs were, which was by incorporation of indigenous knowledge of a substance's efficacy as a curative or preventative for a specific disease. Native Americans did not know of cinchona's powers against malaria because it was a disease Europeans and Africans had only recently introduced to the Americas.

The cinchona tree did not even flourish in the kind of wet, hot region that fostered malaria. Instead it was found in the relatively dry foothills of the Andes, where Native Americans took its bark as a curative for shivering. Around 1630, Jesuits and other Catholic missionaries in the area grew interested in the bark's possibilities as a cure for malaria or at least something to treat the shivering fits associated with the disease.

------

[3]The active ingredient in cinchona, quinine, is still commonly prescribed both as a cure and a preventative for malaria.

The "Jesuit's bark" or "Peruvian bark" traveled the Jesuit network to Rome, where it arrived in 1631. The new drug found a champion in the Jesuit Cardinal Juan de Lugo (1583–1660), director of the Vatican pharmacy. The new drug had cured De Lugo himself of the recurring malaria that plagued him, and he took the initiative to distribute the drug among the poor and other malaria sufferers of the city. The remedy was not a miracle cure, however, and not all medical authorities in Europe accepted it. In particular, many European Protestants were initially reluctant to adopt a remedy associated with the hated Jesuits.

Despite resistance, the relative success of the drug increased the demand for it. The Jesuit pharmacy in Lima, Peru, eventually became the world center for the preparation and distribution of cinchona bark.

"CREOLE" JESUITS AND THE DEBATE OVER THE NEW WORLD

By the eighteenth century, many Spanish-American Jesuits originated in "Creole" communities. Creoles were the descendants of earlier Spanish immigrants. One of the fundamental social conflicts of the time was between the Creoles and the "Peninsulares" or "Gachupines," immigrants from Spain who held many of the political and religious offices of the colonies, as well as providing the merchants and traders who controlled much of the economy. The Peninsulares often had the support of the Spanish government, which from the early days of the conquest had been suspicious of the loyalty Creoles felt for the Spanish crown.

One of the differences between Creoles and Peninsulares, a stereotype that went back to the sixteenth century, was the peninsular belief that Creoles were unfit for government because they had been "softened" by the climate of the Americas. In the eighteenth century, this argument was broadened by European natural historians into one that maintained that the entire biology of the New World was inferior to that of the old. Particularly important for New World natural historians was defending the reputation of the Western hemisphere from European scientists like the French natural historian, the Comte du Buffon (1707–1788). Buffon pointed to cases where New World animals were smaller than those of the Old World, as pumas were smaller than lions, to argue that the New World, for reasons of climate and humidity, produced generally inferior fauna. Animals that should be large, such as mammals, were smaller, while animals that should be small, like insects and frogs, were bigger. Moreover, Old World animals degenerated in the Americas. Buffon was the most famous zoologist of the eighteenth century, so his argument could not be dismissed.

Buffon's argument was expanded and amplified by a Dutch scholar, Cornelius de Pauw, author of *Philosophical Researches on the Americans or Memoirs for the History of the Human Species* (1768). De Pauw wrote in French, the international language of learning in Europe at that time, and his work attracted widespread interest throughout the continent. De Pauw's most important contribution to the debate was extending Buffon's claims about the inferiority of American animals into claims of the inferiority of American people. Nature in America was not immature, as Buffon described it, it was senile. Native Americans were not merely inferior in culture but biologically inferior as well, smaller, weaker, and less intelligent than Europeans. Native American women were so ugly as to be indistinguishable from native men. In fact, De Pauw suggested that Native Americans were not really human at all. Although his principal focus was on people, De Pauw drew heavily on Buffon to suggest that the inferior environment of the Americas affected animals as well, both those indigenous to America and those imported there—dogs lost their bark, camels their reproductive ability.

The argument on the inferiority of American nature expanded into all kinds of detailed claims, such as that American birds could not sing beautifully like the nightingale of Europe. Some made great play with the beardlessness of Native Americans or Native men's purportedly lower sex drive in comparison with European men. The most controversial claim made by Europeans gave a new scientific gloss to the old anti-Creole prejudices by asserting that Europeans themselves inevitably degenerated in the Americas. This aroused the pride of New World scientists in both North and South America.[4]

Closed off from many positions of public trust, sons of the Creole elite often made their way into religious orders, including the Jesuits. This "creolization" of the society in Latin America had a profound effect on its culture. While Acosta had seen the richness of the New World in terms of the resources available to the Spanish monarchy, eighteenth-century Creole Jesuits, like other Creoles, viewed their primary political loyalty as to their *patria*, or fatherland, be it

---

[4]North America's leading eighteenth-century scientist, Benjamin Franklin, was likewise a champion of New World fauna, as was his fellow-rebel Thomas Jefferson.

Mexico, Peru, or one of the smaller provinces of the Spanish Empire, such as Chile. Many Jesuits wrote natural and political histories of the places where they lived, often emphasizing the development of the Native American societies that preceded the Spanish conquerors.

However, Creoles, of European descent and Christians themselves, could not fully identify or proclaim themselves as the heirs of the pre-Columbian civilizations and societies their ancestors had destroyed or altered. One alternative was identification not with the history, but with the nature of their "patrias." Creoles praised the abundance, health, and wealth of their lands, making exactly the opposite claims to those of Buffon, De Pauw, and other European naturalists. Some works by Creoles, included discussions of natural history meant to disprove the assertions of Buffon and Pauw.

Many Creole Jesuits were uprooted from their homes and exiled to Europe by the suppression of the Jesuit order in Spain and the Spanish Empire in 1767. The government's ruthless campaign against the Jesuits only increased their alienation from the Spanish monarchy. Although few of the Spanish-American Jesuits ever saw their homelands again, many kept their loyalty to them.

The expelled Jesuits in Europe were exposed to the widespread and vehement support for the Buffon-De Pauw thesis in intellectual circles. Burning with indignation both toward the abusers of their fatherlands and those "enlightened" Europeans who had driven them from those fatherlands in miserable exile, the Jesuits poured forth a stream of works defending America. The Mexican Father Francesco Saverio Clavigero's four volume *Ancient History of Mexico* (1780–1781), included extensive discussion of Mexico's lands, flora, and fauna, along with a history of its peoples and states. ("Civil history" and "natural history" were still viewed as closely related disciplines by many, as they had been by Acosta.) Clavigero praised the sweet song of Mexican birds, rebutting European claims that American birds could not sing, and the abundance and hardihood of American crops like corn and chocolate. Nor were America's natives the physical weaklings De Pauw described; Clavigero had seen them carry heavy burdens, burdens heavy enough to amaze a European philosopher like De Pauw, whom Clavigero invoked by name, if De Pauw had ever come to America to witness it.

Father Giovanni Ignazio Molina (1740–1829), a Creole Jesuit from Chile, published a *Natural History of Chile* (1782) which also boasted of America's abundant fauna, as well as raging against De

Pauw. Like Clavigero, Molina drew on personal experience, as well as the writings of previous authors, including Acosta. He pointed out that Buffon never visited the Americas himself, and relied on unreliable travelers' accounts. European naturalists also made mistakes by not taking American nature on its own terms, but instead applying European names without regard for whether the American plants and animals they were describing were really the same as the Old World creatures.

ROME: CENTER OF THE JESUIT SCIENTIFIC WORLD

The center of the Jesuit Order in the seventeenth century was its headquarters in Rome. The same was true of Jesuit science. Correspondence, as well as scientific instruments and collections of items, passed through the city, and the Collegio Romano stood at the apex of Jesuit educational institutions. The Collegio moved from its originally cramped quarters to a spacious new building in 1584 through the patronage of Gregory XIII, thereby acquiring a new identity—the Pontifical Gregorian University, or Gregorianum. Logic, natural philosophy, and mathematics played a central role in the Gregorian University's curriculum—a curriculum that was basically scholastic but, nevertheless, innovative. Christoph Clavius, an alumnus of the Collegio as well as a professor, ran an informal group for advanced mathematical and astronomical study at the Gregorian University in the early seventeenth century, and attempted to mediate the disputes between mathematicians and natural philosophers. The Collegio/Gregorianum was also a preeminent center for astronomy in the Catholic world. Galileo was influenced early in his career by the logic and mechanics taught at the Collegio and was honored for his telescopic discoveries with a solemn convocation there in 1611. Astronomers there built astronomical telescopes shortly after Galileo and independently of him, and Rome-based Jesuits played a prominent role in the church's rejection of Galileo's Copernicanism.

Rome was a center for many Jesuit scientific activities other than astronomy. Peruvian bark was not the only new medicine that made its way to the Jesuits in Rome. Rhubarb, bezoar stone,[5] and many

---

[5]An undigested mass found in the gastrointestinal system of grass-eating animals and used as an antidote to poison and as a cure for disease.

other things were sent there. For some of these materials, Rome would be a final home, but natural objects made their way from the city as well as to it. Curiosities and valuable objects could be sent as gifts to smooth the way of Jesuit and Catholic diplomacy. The Collegio/Gregorianum was frequently visited by distinguished visitors to Rome and was the first institutional home of the museum of the mid-seventeenth-century Jesuit scientific star, Athanasius Kircher (1601–1680).

ATHANASIUS KIRCHER AND GLOBAL SCIENCE

Athanasius Kircher, a German Jesuit, was appointed professor of mathematics, physics, and oriental languages on his arrival in Rome in 1633 and remained associated with the Gregorianum after he resigned from his position eight years later. Kircher was a polymath, a Renaissance intellect in the grand style. Humanism, magnetism, optics, Egyptology, astronomy, mathematics, chemistry, and sinology did not exhaust the range of his interests. Kircher's position in European science was not only based on his great intellectual gifts and formidable energy, but also on his location at the center of the worldwide Jesuit scientific network. Because he spent his career in Rome, he was in a uniquely advantageous position to gather observations of astronomical and geophysical phenomena, as well as items, specimens, and curiosities from the vast portion of the globe encompassed by the Jesuits. Kircher's reputation also benefited from the needs of the society, which deliberately promoted him as a leading scientist and scholar. While most Jesuits published under pseudonyms to discourage the sin of pride, all of Kircher's work appeared under his own name.

Kircher published over 40 books, many of them massive illustrated tomes of over a thousand pages. His *Sinica* was one of the first European books on China and drew from the work of Jesuits there. In his youth, Kircher had wanted to go to China as a missionary, but his superiors believed his intellect would do the society greater good in Rome. Kircher's most famous work was his study of ancient Egyptian hieroglyphics. Hieroglyphics had not yet been deciphered, and their real meanings were unknown to anyone. Kircher treated hieroglyphics as complex symbols revealing the ancient holy truths of theology and philosophy handed down from Eden and known to the

Frontispiece of *Mundus Subterraneus* by Athanasius Kircher. *Bibliotheque Nationale, Paris, France/The Bridgeman Art Library International*

Egyptians. His Egyptian studies, along with much else, were given to the world in the massive *Oedipus Aegyptiacus* (1652–1654) which made him a European celebrity. The subsequent true deciphering of Egyptian hieroglyphics, largely by Jean-François Champollion in the early nineteenth century, however, revealed that Kircher's "translations" were totally fanciful.

Like many medieval and early modern European natural philosophers, Kircher viewed his science as an effort to recover ancient wisdom. The assumption was that the scientific, intellectual, and even spiritual traditions of different societies were harmonious with each other and ultimately with Roman Catholicism. He described *Oedipus Aegyptiacus* as replete with "Egyptian wisdom, Phoenician theology, Chaldean astrology, Hebrew cabbala, Persian magic, Pythagorean mathematics, Greek theosophy, mythology, Arabic alchemy, and Latin philology." Careful examination of the words and deeds of all the wise men and prophets of the civilizations of antiquity would reveal that all pointed to fulfillment in the Catholic Church. But Kircher broadened the tradition of ancient wisdom. The dominant view of ancient wisdom in the Renaissance was that it had stemmed from Egypt and was passed on through the Jews, Greeks, Persians, and perhaps Indians to eventually become the heritage of Christian civilization. Kircher, drawing on the work of Jesuit and other scholars across the world, was able to add other civilizations to this story, extending over the Americas and the farthest reaches of Asia, rather than being limited to the Middle East, North Africa, and Europe. Like many others, however, Kircher identified the ancient Egyptians as the ultimate human source of knowledge, and he traced the intellectual development of Chinese and Native Americans, as well as Babylonians and Greeks, to early contacts with Egypt. Chinese characters and Aztec pictographs were both descendants of Egyptian hieroglyphics. Careful study of these writing systems, along with numerous others, could lead to the creation of a new and more accurate universal language, if not the reconstruction of the original language Adam had used to name the beasts.

Natural knowledge, too, was a large part of this synthesis and Kircher firmly believed that the study of nature was a route to the knowledge of God. Kircher was particularly interested in magnetism as a natural force. He saw it as permeating the universe, and a sign and aspect of God's unseen power in maintaining the world. As was common among Jesuits, Kircher also treated light as an emblem of God's power, and wrote a treatise on the subject, *The Great Art of Light and Shadow*. Kircher was not particularly known as an optical theorist, but as an expert in magic lanterns, the casting of shadows, and optical illusions.

Kircher's correspondence extended well out of Europe. His books were very popular in New Spain, and his work on magnetism was written as a present for a Mexican Jesuit and Kircher fan named Alejandro Favian. Another admirer was Sor Juana Inés de la Cruz

(1651–1695), a nun and the greatest poet of colonial Mexico. (Kircher was particularly fond of his Mexican correspondents' gifts of chocolate, a New World product just beginning to become widely known in Europe.) Nor was Kircher's audience limited to Jesuits or even Catholics. He also had a long association and correspondence with the German Lutheran astronomer Johannes Hevelius (1611–1687)—a relationship between a Jesuit and a Protestant that would have been unimaginable in Ignatius's time. Kircher's publisher, Jansson, operated not from the Catholic city of Rome but from Amsterdam, capital of the Protestant Dutch Republic.

As noted, Kircher's position at Rome was quite useful for information gathering. Kircher had access to the finest network of worldwide data gatherers and observers Not only did he receive correspondence from Jesuits scattered all over the world, he could also meet with the many who returned from their far-flung abodes to Jesuit headquarters in the Eternal City. In return, Jesuits carried his books with them on their journeys throughout the world. Even though many of Kircher's books were gigantic, their encyclopedic range made them valuable in their portability. A single Kircher tome took the place of a library of natural philosophy. Kircher's reputation extended far and wide due to his voluminous correspondence and the global reach of the Catholic Church and the Jesuits, making him the first scientist to achieve worldwide fame in the scientific community.

Kircher's massive volumes were complemented by the enormous collection of unusual natural and artificial objects, the greatest in Europe, at the Jesuits' Gregorianum. The collection was known, after its curator, as the Musaeum Kircherianum. Collecting all kinds of things—ingenious mechanical and optic devices, ancient coins, stuffed animals, horns, and hides—was a common practice among the European elite, and the size and quality of objects in a collection made a statement about the collector. The variety of objects in this collection was evidence of the global reach and power of the Catholic Church and the Society of Jesus. The museum was one of the few places where Europeans could see stuffed and preserved specimens of the "exotic" animals of the Americas. Particularly eminent visitors would be guided around the collection by Kircher himself, who also performed elegant experiments and demonstrations for the pleasure and edification of his guests. Rome's place as a center of ecclesiastical business and Catholic pilgrimage ensured that the museum would receive many visitors from many countries, and as religious passions cooled Protestants too came in increasing numbers to see the sights of the ancient city as well as Kircher's collection.

THE DECLINE OF JESUIT SCIENCE

Despite his towering influence, by the time of Kircher's death in the late seventeenth century the Society of Jesus was clearly no longer a leader in European science. The Jesuits' rejection of Copernican astronomy made them increasingly an anachronism, while their adherence to Aristotelian physics also left them behind, as scientists turned to the new physical systems of Rene Descartes and Isaac Newton. Jesuit centralization in Rome was also dragging down the society's ability to participate in science, as Rome and the papacy were less important in the century following the condemnation of Galileo and the rise of new centers of patronage in Protestant Europe and Catholic France, where there was more money and intellectual freedom. Some of the luster of papal patronage was lost, as Louis XIV of France became Europe's premier patron in the sciences, as in many other fields. Jesuits, including the French Jesuit missionaries in China, also enjoyed Louis's patronage but they were excluded from the most important scientific organizations of the later seventeenth century. The French Royal Academy of Sciences barred Jesuits, due to what was considered their dogmatic Aristotelianism. Europe's other leading scientific organization, Protestant Britain's Royal Society, although it admitted Catholic laity, excluded members of religious orders and priests.

The intellectual and cultural style of Jesuit science was also increasingly anachronistic. Despite his skepticism regarding alchemy and natural magic, and his interest in experiment and new instruments, such as the microscope, even Kircher gained a reputation among late seventeenth-century scientists, particularly Protestant ones, as highly credulous and even a laughingstock. Scientists in the active northern European scientific centers of France, England, and the Netherlands treated Jesuits not as natural-philosophical authorities but as useful gatherers of information. Even as gatherers of information, the Jesuits were increasingly outshone by the network of scientific societies created in the eighteenth century and centering on London's Royal Society and Paris's Royal Academy of Sciences. The Jesuits played only a secondary role in the most important scheme for

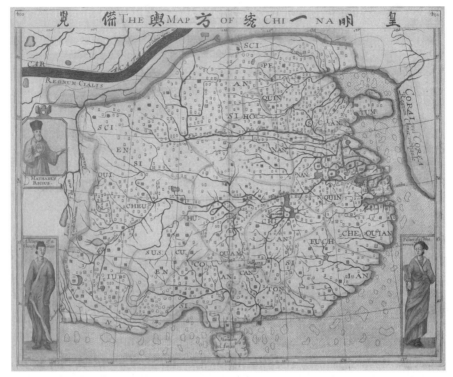

Jesuit Map of China with inset portraits of Matteo Ricci and two costumed figures c. 1625–1626. *Private Collection/The Bridgeman Art Library International*

coordinated observations in the eighteenth century, the observations of the transits of Venus across the face of the Sun in 1761 and 1769.

Jesuit science also suffered in the eighteenth century from the general hostility many governments from China to Brazil displayed toward the society. As one of the most powerful of the international Catholic religious orders, the Jesuits suffered as the secularization of politics made religion less important than national interests. The society was dissolved in France and its dominions in 1764 and banned from Spain and its possessions in 1767. The Jesuit house at Lima was suppressed by Spanish troops, and the pharmacy disappeared a few years later. The pope, under pressure from Catholic rulers, suppressed the Jesuits in 1773 (and the order would only be reconstituted in 1814). Word did not reach China until 1774, when Michel Benoist, the Jesuit who had introduced Copernican heliocentrism to China, died of heartbreak.

SOURCES

■ João Rodrigues on East Asian Cosmology and Physics

The Portuguese João Rodrigues (1558–1633), one of the earliest Jesuit missionaries to East Asia, made his way to Asia, never to return, at the age of 15. In 1580 he entered the Jesuit Order in Japan, and he was ordained a priest in 1596. The earlier part of his missionary career was spent in Japan, where he studied the language and culture closely and became intimate with some of the country's most powerful leaders. In 1610 he was expelled from Japan, and spent the rest of his missionary career in China, based at the Portuguese community at Macao. Selected by his Jesuit superior to draft a history of the order's mission in Japan, Rodrigues began the never-finished project with a look at Japanese culture's roots in Buddhism and Chinese thought.

In this passage he describes East Asian cosmology, contrasting it to European Christian thought. How does Rodrigues relate Asian beliefs to European? How does he present disagreements among Chinese thinkers? According to him, what was the relationship in East Asian thought between science and "magic," such as astrology? All things considered, how did he view the worth of East Asian science?

The Chinese, and also the Japanese who received them from them, divide their sciences into two categories. The first is natural magic, which deals with the production of the universe, the origins of natural things, the generation and corruption of things, fate, judicial[6] and genethliacal[7] astronomy.[8] . . . The second is astronomy, which deals with the Heavens. . . .

They divide astronomy into speculative and practical. Speculative astronomy deals with the structure of the upper and lower world; the Heavens and their movements; the rising and setting of the celestial signs and planets; the material sphere and its circles; the conjunctions of the planets and eclipses of the Sun and moon; the planetary hours and time, and, after their fashion, everything else in this field that our astronomers also study. Practical astrology, which others call judicial, prognostic, and also divinatory, deals with good and bad days to work, and other contingent things that can be foretold by the celestial appearances and aspects, and the conjunctions of the planets among themselves and the stars.

---

[6]Using the stars to predict the future or answer questions.
[7]The determination of a person's character or future by the position of the stars at their birth.
[8]What we would call astrology.

As regards the unity of the world, we believe according to our faith that there is only one world. This is in keeping with natural reason that shows it to be so and at the same time shows that both the Earth and sky are round in shape. Just as there were various theories held by ancient philosophers concerning the unity and form of the world, so also here among those of the sects. Some believe there to be only one world, others say that there are almost infinitely many. Some say that it is shaped this way, others say that way. Some say that Earth is square with six sides and the sky is round and fluid; others say it is pyramidal, high and low, with many heavens like worlds. We put here briefly what these philosophers hold over here, remarking in the first place that our philosophers who held this opinion probably took it from the sages of these parts, just as they took other theories, principally from the Indian sect and that of the Chaldeans [ancient Mesopotamians], which is the same as the sect of the Chinese astrological scholars. The reason from this is that the philosophers of these parts lived long before the others and even before the Greek philosophers. . . .

The Chinese philosophers postulate only one world, consisting of Heaven and Earth. They believe that Heaven is round and Earth is square, surrounded on its four sides by four seas and situated in the middle of or within the sky. So on account of its shape, they say that it is motionless and only the upper part or surface is inhabited. The Japanese follow this theory, and accordingly divide the structure of the world into celestial and terrestrial, or superior and inferior. The first is expressed by the word "Heaven" which they call *ten*, or *tian* in Chinese. They understand by this word all the ethereal and aerial world, the sky, stars, planets, the Heavenly influences, its five elements or five elementary qualities, that is, fire, wood, Earth, water, and metal.

According to their explanation, these correspond . . . with hot, cold, dry and wet. These are called elements, and they place them in the region of the air or ether, supported in the substance of the air in their appropriate places; fire in the south, water in the north, wood in the east, metal in the west, and Earth in the middle. They believe that these qualities correspond to the properties of the five planets: wood to Jupiter, fire to Mars, Earth to Saturn, metal to Venus, water to Mercury, and so they call these planets by these names. The Sun and moon are like a source and include these five qualities: the Sun, hot and dry; the moon, wet and cold.

The second region is expressed by the word *chi*, or *di* in Chinese, that is, Earth, by which they understand land, seas, rivers, lakes, stones, metals, trees, and all the rest contained therein. They believe that Earth is visible, and that water and fire are not elements but are compounds that are generated and corrupt like everything else corporeal. They maintain this because the elements cannot be generated or corrupted, for they are the ingredients of which things are composed and into which they resolve by the corruption of the compound, and one is not generated from another.

Rodrigues, João, *João Rodrigues's Account of Sixteenth-century Japan*, ed. Michael Cooper (London: Hakluyt Society, 2001), 357–361.

■ José de Acosta, *Of the Naturall and Moral History of the Indies*

José de Acosta was the leading natural historian of the Spanish Empire in the sixteenth century. Born in Castile to a merchant family, he showed an early interest in the Americas. After joining the Jesuits, he petitioned his superiors to be sent to the Americas or Africa. Acosta arrived in Lima in 1572, and remained in America until 1586, serving as "provincial," or head, of the Jesuits in Peru from 1576 to 1581. He published three books on the Americas, all supporting the Jesuit and Catholic missionary effort in the Spanish possessions. His *Natural and Moral History of the Indies* covered both the natural resources and the indigenous peoples of Peru and Mexico.

Acosta's choice to write in Spanish rather than Latin indicated that his audience was Spanish churchmen and intellectuals rather than a European-wide audience of the learned. However, before his death, Acosta's books were published in Dutch, French, Italian, German, and Latin. The first English translation, which is excerpted here, appeared a few years later, in 1604. The appearance of so many translations of Acosta's work is a remarkable testimony to the internationalism of scholarship and science and to the strength of curiosity about the Americas. At this time, merely for a Jesuit to set foot in England rendered him liable to the death penalty.

What does Acosta see as the goal of his science? How does he relate his work to the classic works of ancient scientists? For what reasons is the work of "benefite" to readers?

Everie naturall Historie is of it selfe pleasing, and very profitable, to such as will raise up their discourse and contemplation on high, in that it doth move them to glorify the Author of all Nature, as we see the wise and holy men do, specially David[9] in many Psalmes. And Job likewise, treating of the secrets of the Creator, whereas the same Lord answereth Job so amplie.[10] He that takes delight to understand the wondrous works of Nature shal taste the true pleasure and content of Histories; and the more, whenas he shall know they are not the simple workes of men, but of the Creator himself, and that he shall comprehend the naturall causes of these workes, then shall he truly occupie himself in the studie of Philosophie. But he that shall raise his consideration higher, beholding the gret and first architect of all these marvells, he shal know his wisedom and infinite greatnes, and (we may say) shall be divinely imployed. And so the discourse of naturall things may serve for many good considerations, although the feeblenes and weaknes of many appetites are commonly accustomed to stay at things less profitable, which is the desire to know new things, called curiositie. The Discourse and Historie of naturall things of the Indies (besides the common content it gives) hath yet another benefite, which is to treate of things a farre off, the greatest part whereof were unknowne to the most excellent Authors of that profession which have been among the Ancients. And if wee should write these naturall things of the Indies so amply as they require, being so strange, I doubt not but we might compile works no less than those of Plinie, Theophrastus, and Aristotle.[11] But I hold not my selfe sufficient, and although I were, yet is not my intent but to note some naturall things which I have seene and knowne being at the Indies, or have received from men worthy of credit, the which seeme rare to me and scarce known in Europe. By reason whereof I will pass over many of them briefly, ether bicause they are writen of by others, or else require a longer discourse than I can now give.

Acosta, José de, *Natural and Moral History of the Indies, by Father Joseph de Acosta, reprinted from the English translated edition of Edward Grimston, 1604, and edited, with notes and an introduction, by Clements R. Markham*, Two Volumes (London: Hakluyt Society, 1880), Volume I, 104–105.

■ Matteo Ricci on Using Science in China

Father Matteo Ricci's *The True Meaning of the Lord of Heaven*, published in Beijing in 1603, was a tract arguing for a Christian concept of God and creation in the language of classical Chinese philosophy. It is

---

[9]The biblical book of Psalms was believed to be the work of David, an ancient king of Israel.
[10]A reference to the biblical book of Job.
[11]Pliny, Theophrastus, and Aristotle were all ancient natural historians.

written in the form of a dialogue between a Western scholar, Ricci's stand-in, and a Chinese Confucian scholar.

One of Ricci's tasks was to impress on Chinese readers the power of God as a creator, as traditional Chinese thought did not use the concept of creation. This required assertions about the nature of the created world. Ricci argues for the existence of a human soul against what he views as the materialistic tendency of Confucian thought. This leads him to emphasize the differences between humans and animals.

How do the Chinese and Western pictures of nature, as presented by Ricci, differ? Textbooks usually characterize such dominant schools of Chinese thought as Daoism and Neo-Confucianism as "non-dualistic." What does this mean? As presented here, is Chinese thought non-dualistic? What arguments does the Western scholar use? Can Western scientific or, for that matter, religious thought be non-dualistic? How does the debate relate to the religious issues that underlay Ricci's writings?

The Chinese Scholar Says: Although it is said that heaven, Earth, and all phenomena share one material energy, the forms and images of things are, nevertheless, different, and for this reason they are divided into a variety of categories. The human body may simply appear as a physical body, but both within it and outside it there is the material energy of Yin and Yang[12] which fills heaven and Earth. Through creation material energy becomes all things,[13] and because of the existence of categories, things become different from one another. It is like fish in water; the water outside the fish is the same as the water in the fish's stomach; the water in the stomach of a mandarin fish is the same as the water in the stomach of a carp. It is only the appearances of the fish which persist in being different, so that the fish fall into separate categories. One has only to look at the differing forms and appearances of all the things in the world to be able to know each of the different categories.

The Western Scholar Says: To distinguish between things on the basis of appearance is not to distinguish between the various categories of

[12]The basic opposing but necessarily complementary elements of existence: Yin is weak, yielding, female, dark, and moist; Yang is strong, assertive, male, light, and dry. Their dynamic equilibrium creates a unity.
[13]This is known to Neo-Confucians as *qi* (pronounced "chee"), the flow of energy or life force that infuses everything.

things, but only between their external appearances. External appearances are not the things themselves. If one distinguishes between things on the basis of their appearances rather than on the basis of their natures, then must not the nature of dogs be regarded as being the same as the nature of oxen, and the natures of dogs and oxen be regarded as being the same as human nature? . . . If one moulds a tiger and a man out of clay it is appropriate to assert that only their external appearances are dissimilar; but it is definitely not appropriate to say of a living tiger and a living man that only their looks are different. If one distinguishes between things on the basis of their appearances, and these are largely alike, it will not be possible to place them in separate categories. If one takes the example of the clay tiger and the clay man, however, although their external appearances are very different from each other, they must both be classified as clay.

If material energy is regarded as spirit and the basis of life, how can living things ever die? If, after living things have died, they continue to be imbued with and surrounded by material energy, where can they go to escape material energy? How can one die from any disaster that it not material in character? Therefore, material energy is not the basis of life.

■ Athanasius Kircher on Earthquakes

Athanasius Kircher was particularly interested in geoscience. On one of his few trips outside Rome, he had himself lowered into Mt. Etna, the Sicilian volcano. His *Mundus Subterraneous* was one of the most influential works on geoscience in the mid-seventeenth century. This passage, translated into English in 1669 for a pamphlet on earthquakes, gives a vivid picture of the subterranean world.

How does Kircher describe natural processes? What underlies his confidence about the nature of the underground world, given that he has not seen it? How does his scientific argument relate to his beliefs about God?

The central Fire A, through certain Fire-Ducts, or Channels, diffuses round about, everywhere, far and near fiery exhalations or spirits. These Driven into the Waterhouses, it partly disposes into Hot Baths;

partly attenuates or rarifies into vapours, which dashing, as it were, against the Arches, or Vaults, of Concavous Dens, and condens'd by the coldness of the place, and lastly dissolved into Waters, generate Fountains and Rivers; and then partly derived into fit Matrices and Receptacles, fruitful of other kind of Juyces, of several Minerals, contract fast together, and harden into Metallick Bodies; or else are ordered for a new Conception, and fructifying of combustible Matter, to nourish, and still feed and maintain the Fire. You see there also, how the Sea, by the Winds and pressure of the Air, or motion of the aestuating Tides, ejaculate and cast forth the Waters, through Subterraneous, or underground Burrows, into the highest Waterhouses of the Mountains. You see also the Sea and the Plains in the utmost surface of the Earth, to take place next to the Subterraneous World; and the Air next to them, as the Scheme teaches: Yet you are not to imagine, that the Fires and Waters, &c. are really thus disposed in Nature underground. For whoever has seen them? But this onely was to signifie, according to the best Imagination of the Author, that they are after some well-ordered and artificial, or organiz'd way or other, contriv'd by Nature; and that the Under-ground World is a well fram'd House, with distinct Rooms, Cellars, and Store-Houses, by great Art and Wisdom fitted together; and not, as many think, a confused and jumbled heap or Chaos of things, as it were, of Stones, Bricks, Wood, and other Materials, as the rubbish of a decayed House, or an House not yet Made.

The volcano's, or, Burning and fire-vomiting mountains famous in the world, with their remarkables collected for the most part out of Kircher's Subterraneous world; and exposed to more general view in English . . . , (London: Printed by J. Darby for John Allen . . . 1669), iii.

CHAPTER 3

Westernization, "Modernization," and Science in Russia and Japan, 1684–1860s

One of the most important developments in the history of world science has been the spread of the scientific ideas and practices developed in Europe to other societies, a phenomenon caused by both "push" and "pull" factors. European political domination or missionary efforts, like those of the Jesuits, have introduced Western science into, and even imposed it on, other societies. However, some non-Western societies have studied or adopted European science for their own purposes. Two of the most interesting cases of this "pull" phenomenon occurred in eighteenth- and early nineteenth-century Russia and Japan. No non-Western society in that period took as much interest in Western science as did those two countries. Both assumed a favorable attitude toward Western science in the early eighteenth century, but were not full-fledged members of the international scientific community for nearly a century-and-a-half later. The two countries also faced similar problems in ensuring that science was not accompanied by "dangerous" political and religious ideas. There were, however, also huge differences between the Japanese and Russian cases.

In Russia, the introduction of science was part of an effort by elites, initially led by Tsar Peter the Great (reign 1682–1725), to make their culture more "Western." This effort involved many other areas besides science, and was accompanied by a political and cultural opening to the West and efforts to attract Western scientists to settle and work in Russia. However, the autocratic Russian government was always concerned to prevent the introduction of subversive political ideas, either of a British-style constitutional monarchy or the revolutionary democracy of the French Revolution. The filters that various imperial Russian regimes imposed on Western ideas varied in severity, but they often affected the ability of Russian scientists to communicate with their colleagues in the West.

The Japanese had far less direct contact with Westerners than the Russians or many other non-Western peoples, such as the Chinese and the Ottoman Turks, who, however, displayed much less interest in Western science. The Tokugawa dynasty of shoguns had shut the islands off from the outside world in the seventeenth century. The only point of contact between Japan and the West was a Dutch trading post on a small artificial island, Deshima, in the harbor of Nagasaki. But paradoxically, by cutting off Westerners' access to Japan, Japanese authorities opened the possibility of a far deeper cultural penetration by Western science. When the Chinese or Russian governments wanted Western technical expertise they could hire Westerners, like the Jesuit heads of the Astronomical Bureau at Beijing or the Germans, French, and Swiss who filled the Imperial Academy of Sciences at St. Petersburg, but if the Japanese wanted to employ Western knowledge, they would have to learn it themselves. The Japanese also differed from the Russians in that the government was concerned to limit the cultural and social, as well as the political, impact of Western science, rather than using it as part of a program of social transformation. As already noted, Russian elites viewed science as part of a project of social, cultural, and technological Westernization; the Japanese viewed Westernization as a danger. Both, however, feared that science might introduce Western ideas of limited or republican government.

SCIENCE AND STATE-DRIVEN WESTERNIZATION IN RUSSIA

Science in Russia Before Peter the Great

There was little scientific literature available in pre-Petrine Russia and no scientific institutions. Its religion was Orthodox Christianity, much less friendly to science than other religious traditions, including Roman Catholicism and Islam. The main learned language of Russia and the Orthodox Slavic world, Church Slavonic, was tightly focused on religion. Unlike Latin, the language of the Roman Catholic Church, Church Slavonic produced neither original scientific literature nor translations from Greek science beyond the extremely elementary. Nor was there science in Russia's other major written language, the "chancery Russian" of government officials. The Russian church and state did not create intellectual institutions like the universities of Catholic and Protestant Europe. What few printed books appeared were nearly all devoted to religious topics. Technical experts from the West, including architects, physicians, and military officers, brought some knowledge with them, but they usually came and went without training Russian successors, and their efforts did not lead to a scientific culture or technical or scientific institutions in Russia itself. Foreigners, usually Germans, recruited to build and run workshops and mills, remained in their enclaves separate from Russian life, and were viewed as heretical enemies by ordinary Orthodox Russians. So isolated was Russia from Western scientific developments that Russians did not even use Arabic numerals, using instead an older and far less flexible Greek system, in which letters of the alphabet stood for numbers. Changing geographical knowledge also had little impact on Russians. The existence of the Americas was not referred to in a printed Russian book until 1710, when it appeared in the first Russian geography textbook.

Science and Westernization in the Reign of Peter the Great

Tsar Peter I the Great (reign 1682–1725) had as much impact, both short- and long-term, on his country as any ruler in world history. He was undoubtedly more responsible than anyone else for the introduction of Western science into Russia. Bringing science to the country, however, was only part of Peter's "cultural revolution from above" designed to transform the culture of Russia's elite. The first Russian Tsar to travel to Western Europe, Peter felt a great personal affinity with Western European culture, while fully exploiting the Russian political tradition of despotism to impose the new ideas and organizations. Western science met with surprisingly little resistance in Peter's time, simply because Peter did not permit it.

The principal driving force of Peter's modernization campaign was the preservation and military expansion of the Russian state. Peter was an aggressive imperialist, who fought wars with Russia's traditional enemies, Sweden and Poland, as well as the Ottoman Empire. Obsessed with ships and sailing from his youth, Peter was particularly interested in building a strong navy—a major challenge in a country without a warm-water harbor or a naval tradition. His wars with the Swedes and Turks, in fact, were aimed at increasing Russian access to the Baltic and Black Seas. The introduction of a modern navy on the Western model required extensive science and technological expertise. Navigation relied on advanced astronomy and mathematics. Sailors also required accurate cartographical and hydrographical charts.

The need for trained navigators led to the founding of Russia's first institution of higher learning outside of its theological seminaries, the Moscow School of Mathematics and Navigation founded in 1701. State-sponsored mathematical and astronomical institutions with an emphasis on nautical applications were common throughout Europe, and Peter's new school of advanced studies drew on the resources of England, the country with the most technically advanced and powerful navy of the period. Its first teachers were three Britons hired by Peter on his visit to England. In 1715, the upper level of the school was moved to Peter's new capital of St. Petersburg on the Baltic, where it became the Russian Naval Academy.

The work of Naval Academy teachers went far beyond the navy. They were largely responsible for the introduction of Arabic numerals to Russia, and the mathematical education they offered trained not just navigators but the surveyors and cartographers responsible for the first modern map of the enormous Russian Empire.

Although the task of modernizing Russia's land forces did not require nearly the technical demands of the navy, there was a considerable body of new knowledge that had to be assimilated. This was particularly true for the engineers who fortified strongholds, conducted sieges, and supervised the use of artillery. Military engineers were always the most scientific, or technically adept, branch of any eighteenth-century European army. The science of ballistics, with its

Peter the Great's Boat. *Library of Congress, Prints & Photographs Division, Prokudin-Gorskii Collection (reproduction number LC-DIG-prok-11401)*

roots in sixteenth-century physics, was devoted to problems associated with delivering accurate shot to a target. Russia's first artillery school, inaugurated in 1698, was connected to Peter's personal regiment, the Praeobrazhenskii Guards. The first Russian artillery regiment, with an associated corps of engineers, was founded three years later.

The introduction of Western science faced resistance from the Russian Orthodox Church. Yet Peter's iron control over the church, the one organization in Russia that could have opposed him effectively, meant that it had little ability to stop the spread in state institutions of heliocentric astronomy and other new principles that challenged traditional Orthodox beliefs. However, the church retained some autonomy, and its own institutions and teachings remained extremely conservative. What little science was taught in its seminaries was based on Aristotelian physics, and it resisted the introduction of heliocentric astronomy into the seminary curriculum.

The Transformation of the Russian Language

The introduction of Western science to Russia presented a fundamental linguistic challenge. In the late seventeenth century, the old international language of Western science, Latin, was declining in favor of increased use of vernacular languages, particularly French. Russians had little knowledge of Latin or other Western languages, and the near nonexistence of Russian science before Peter meant that much of science simply could not be expressed in Russian. The problem was further complicated by the existence of Church Slavonic, more geared toward theological and philosophical discussion than Russian, but rapidly left behind in Peter's revolution. About 4,500 foreign words from various Western languages entered Russian in Peter's reign, including extensive technical vocabularies for navigation and seafaring, as well as military technology. Medicine was another area where Russia absorbed foreign terminology, including *anatomiia* and *medikament*. The Russian mathematical vocabulary was virtually created in Peter's reign, including *matematika* itself, and other scientific terms introduced at this time included *laboratoriia*, *mikroskop*, and *khimiia*.

The creation of scientific Russian was part of a larger effort to make Russian a vehicle for Western culture. This transformation emphasized simplicity, as opposed to the ornateness of Church Slavonic and the pomposity of Chancery Russian. The new Russian was intended to be read by persons lacking the traditional, church-dominated higher education. Many letters considered superfluous were eliminated from the alphabet, essentially creating the modern Cyrillic alphabet.

The Imperial Academy of Sciences of St. Petersburg

The culmination of Peter's efforts to bring Western knowledge and techniques to Russia was the founding of the country's first academy of sciences in 1724, shortly before his death. Scientific academies played a central role in eighteenth-century Western science, forming an international network that could be brought to bear on a number of topics. The most prestigious were France's Royal Academy of Sciences and Britain's Royal Society, both founded in the 1660s. These societies sponsored expeditions and research, set the scientific agenda with the posing of "prize questions," and legitimated scientists by admitting them to membership and publishing their work in affiliated journals.

The early eighteenth century was marked by the creation of scientific societies outside the original capitals of London and Paris, such as Prussia's Berlin Academy, founded in 1700. The founding of a scientific society with state sponsorship was a crucial step toward full participation in the world of international science. Peter had visited both the Royal Society and the Royal Academy of Sciences, and was even admitted as a member of the Royal Academy. He had also corresponded with the German philosopher and polymath Gottfried Wilhelm Leibniz (1646–1716), a keen promoter of scientific academies, who had inspired the founding of the Berlin Academy and had a longstanding interest in Russia.

Unlike the Berlin Academy and other Western institutions, the Imperial Academy of Sciences was a vast complex, including a university, a high school, an observatory, a library, a botanical garden, and a printing press and translation bureau for Western scientific books. The academy had a monopoly on printing almanacs and published Russia's only newspaper, the *St. Petersburg Gazette*. The scientific academy proper, known as the "Archives Conference," was only part of this massive institution, designed to build a Russian scientific culture essentially from scratch. The Archives Conference was built on the model of the Paris Royal Academy of Sciences, with paid academicians, rather than as an amateur group like Britain's Royal Society. The members were divided into twenty academicians and twenty associates, and met weekly. The whole operation was overseen by a government-appointed director and vice director.

The first task in setting up the academy was to recruit European academicians. Sixteen European scholars were recruited to provide its nucleus. Leaders among the first group were the astronomer Joseph-Nicholas Delisle (1688–1768) from France and the mathematicians Nicholas Bernoulli (1695–1726), Daniel Bernoulli (1700–1782), and Jakob Hermann (1678–1733) from Switzerland. Factionalism along national lines, usually pitting the Germans against the Russians and French, would plague the Imperial Academy for decades. Few of the foreign academicians bothered to learn Russian, further alienating them from Russians.

In its early years, the academy suffered from intermittent government support, and its educational institutions withered as the Russian government preferred to send young Russian men to universities in Europe. Nonetheless, the Imperial Academy managed to establish a record of scholarly production. The first volume of *Commentaries* appeared in 1726, and its successors appeared on a regular basis. The academy sought to overcome its isolation by building relationships with other scientific societies. Its strongest early relationship was with the Royal Society, which sent a number of meteorological queries for the Imperial Academy and with which the academy set up an official exchange of publications in 1729. This was the first exchange of publications between scientific societies, and a significant step in building international cooperation.

Given Russia's vast size, and the complete lack of geographical knowledge about much of it, geography and cartography were high on the Imperial Academy's agenda. Much of Russia's huge Siberian territory was essentially unknown to science. The academy sponsored the second expedition of Vitus Bering (1681–1741) from 1732 to 1743. It produced the first map of Russia in 1734, the first Russian atlas in 1745, and published maps of the Pacific in 1758 and 1773.

In 1747, the academy finally received a formal charter, which protected it from some of the worst excesses of the government. In 1749, it launched its first prize competition. Prize competitions were extremely important in eighteenth-century scientific academies, and the fact that the academy could now offer one was a mark of its maturity. The subject of the competition was the relation of variations in the lunar motion to Newtonian physical theory, and the winner was the French mathematical physicist Alexis-Claude Clairaut (1713–1765). The Imperial Academy cooperated with the Paris Academy of Sciences in the observation of the transit of Mercury in 1753, and cosponsored an observation trip to Tobolsk by the French astronomer Jean-Baptiste Chappe d'Auteroche (1722–1769) in connection with the transit of Venus in 1761.[1] For the 1769 transit, the academy sent out eight expeditions, including one to the farthest reaches of Russian Asia in Kamchatka.

---

[1]Transits are those occasions when Venus or Mercury, as viewed from Earth, moves across the face of the Sun. A coordinated series of observations from different points on the Earth surface could help establish the distance of the Earth from the Sun. Transits of Venus are particularly rare.

The academy's high salaries and growing reputation attracted first-class savants (despite the handicap of the Russian weather), such as the German electrical physicist Franz Theodor Ulrich Aepinus (1724–1802), who arrived in 1757, and the Swiss mathematician Leonhard Euler (1707–1783), who spent the years 1727 to 1741 and 1766 to 1783 in St. Petersburg. Conflicts between foreign and Russian-born academicians continued, however, particularly when the Russian faction acquired a distinguished scientist as leader, Mikhail Vasilyevich Lomonosov (1711–1765). In 1758, Lomonosov became head of the academy's influential geographical department. Despite having been educated at the University of Marburg in Germany, he resented the foreign, particularly German, scientists who filled so many positions in the academy. Lomonosov was a proud Russian, who used his considerable poetic skills to encourage young Russians to emulate the great scientists of the European past. He also published a grammar of the Russian language, and helped further advance the development of scientific Russian. Lomonosov's membership in the academy was fraught with political tension, and he was even imprisoned for several months.

One of the major difficulties that the academy faced in comparison to its European contemporaries was the strong control exerted by the imperial government. The academy never managed to establish the independence of the Royal Society or even the institutional weight of the Royal Academy of Sciences. Constant interference by courtiers, often ignorant of or even hostile to science, hampered the academy's development. The marginal position of the academy in European science and its subjection to the autocratic power of the Russian ruler, however, enabled it to make a startling innovation in the late eighteenth century. In 1783, at a time when women were barred from membership of the Royal Society and Royal Academy, as well as most other European scientific academies, Tsarina Catherine II the Great (reign 1762–1796), appointed Princess Ekaterina Dashkova (1743–1810), the first female head of a European scientific society, with a mission to reform the academy.

The French Revolution and Russian Science

In 1789, the French Revolution began. Originally aimed at reforming the French monarchy, the revolution went much farther. The privileges of the nobility were abolished, a republic was declared in 1792, King Louis XVI and Queen Marie Antoinette were publicly executed in 1793, and the French Catholic Church was attacked and a "religion of reason" briefly put in its place. The new republic went to war with the great powers of Europe, including Russia, and its armies proved formidable. The radicalism of the French Revolution provoked a conservative reaction in many European countries. In no country was this truer than Russia, with its autocratic political culture and economy based on the labor of unfree peasants, known as serfs.

The reaction, which began late in the reign of Catherine and continued through that of her successor Paul I (reign 1796–1801), was directed against the ideas of the eighteenth-century European Enlightenment and foreign influence in general. Enlightenment thinkers had greatly valued science, and frequently connected its progress with the relatively less restricted societies of France and Great Britain. The liberal Russian aristocracy, which had grown up in the early reign of Catherine, attempted to combine loyalty to Russia with interest in the new ideas from the West, including science, but this position proved hard to maintain as opposition to the ideas of the French Revolution grew. Russian authorities sought to cut off contact between Russian intellectuals, including scientists, and the West. Liberals were repressed in the reign of Paul, and the academy was marginalized due to poor funding, mismanagement, and hostility from the government.

Although the reign of Paul's successor, Alexander I (reign 1801–1825), was initially marked by some liberalization after Paul's extremely repressive regime, Alexander later moved to repression under the influence of mysticism and a belief in Russia's special spiritual destiny. Many politically influential conservative mystics of this period believed that an overemphasis on science led to materialism and ultimately to political radicalism. Russian authorities counteracted the danger of materialistic science by promoting religious interpretations of natural phenomena. One Russian educator argued that since lightning bolts end in a triangle, they refer to the Christian Holy Trinity. The conservative reaction also resulted in the expulsion of many foreign university professors, and refusal to recruit more as the academic staff was "Russified," which led to a marked decrease in the quality of scientific training at Russian universities.

Autocracy and Russian Science under Nicolas I

Tsar Nicolas I (reign 1825–1855) introduced a regime of bureaucratic repression, without the extreme xenophobia of Paul's reign or the mystic excesses of Alexander's. A strict censorship covering every aspect of Russian publishing was set up. Nicolas's regime also continued the policy of Russifying the universities and strictly monitoring contact with the West, frequently banning young Russians from studying at Western universities. Russian universities were brought under tighter government control, with power taken from university bodies to be placed in the hands of government officials. The government sought to limit education to those students it viewed as politically reliable, most commonly members of the aristocracy and gentry.

The move toward Russification had less impact on the Academy of Sciences, which under S. S. Uvarov, president from 1818 to 1849, regained some of its former prestige. Uvarov and the Russian government generally conceived of the Academy as an institution serving the state through applied science rather than theoretical speculation. Uvarov knew that Russia itself could not produce enough first-rate scholars for the Academy, and revived the practice of looking to Europe, particularly Germany. The great German embryologist and all-round scientist Karl Ernst von Baer (1792–1876) was among those recruited to come to St. Petersburg. Von Baer, who moved to Russia permanently in 1834, threw himself into Russian scientific life, as a leader of two new scientific organizations, the Russian Geographical Society and the Russian Entomological Society. Another German, the astronomer Friedrich Georg Wilhelm von Struve (1793–1864), became head of the new Russian observatory at Pulkovo, near Petersburg, which quickly ascended into the ranks of the world's leading astronomical facilities. Not only the scientific leadership, but also the bulk of the Academy's membership remained foreign in this period, and Russians sometimes referred to it as the "German Academy." Even native-born Russians of German or other non-Russian ancestry faced jealousy from ethnic Russians. Ironically, the greatest Russian scientist of the early nineteenth century, the mathematician and founder of non-Euclidean geometry, Nicolai Lobachevsky (1792–1856), was not a member of the Academy and languished in obscurity at the University of Kazan.

Certain sciences were more ideologically suspect than others. The growth of physiology in Russia was hampered by suspicion on the part of state and church authorities that it led to materialism. Physiology had no place for the soul. Geology, which might cast doubt on the story of biblical creation, was also suspect. Mathematics, in contrast, was viewed as abstract, and largely ignored by state and church.

The wave of European revolutions beginning in 1848 did not reach Russia or exert the disastrous effect on Russian science of the French Revolution of 1789, but it did lead the government to look upon the universities and all organs of independent thought with even greater suspicion. Russian students were once again barred from studying at Western universities, and Russian universities were forbidden to invite Western scholars. The government encouraged the sons of Russian aristocratic families to study at military rather than civilian institutions and militarized the universities. However, natural science was not as severely repressed as were the humanities, which were thought to be replete with dangerous ideas leading to political liberalism and support for the liberation of Russia's serfs.

The Disciplinary Societies

The early nineteenth century in Europe and America saw the rise of scientific societies oriented to particular disciplines, supplementing the national academies, which tried to cover every branch of science and often the humanities as well. Russia participated in this trend. One of its earliest disciplinary societies was the Moscow Society of Naturalists, founded in 1805. The Moscow Society, sponsored by the University of Moscow, filled several important roles in the Russian scientific world. It provided a Moscow alternative to the St. Petersburg Imperial Academy of Sciences. It also served the interests of the Russian state with an intense focus on useful studies of Russian natural resources, agriculture, and economic development. The society had a heavier Russian representation than the academy, and unlike the highly professionalized academy, it served as a meeting place for professional scientists and aristocratic amateurs with an interest in natural history. It published a *Journal of the Society of Naturalists*.

Another scientific society with an emphasis on Russian issues was the Russian Geographical Society. Like other geographical societies in the nineteenth century, it was associated with imperial expansion. Modeled on Britain's Royal Geographical Society, the Russian Geographical Society was founded in 1845 by a group of academicians of German origin but naturalized in Russia. The society was devoted to the physical geography, cartography, and ethnography of the vast Russian Empire. Much of Eastern Russia, including Siberia, still remained virtually unknown to science. The Russian government had sponsored several exploratory expeditions to the East, but the explorers' lack of scientific expertise made many of their results useless. The Geographical Society sponsored expeditions to explore Siberia and founded branches in Tiflis and Irkutsk, as well as sponsoring several publications. However, the close association of the society with the Russian imperial project contributed to suspicion of the many Germans who appeared among its membership, even though many ethnic Germans were Russian subjects, members of the Baltic German aristocracy. Not only conservative Russian nationalists were suspicious of the Germans, liberal Russians who hoped to use the society as an instrument of social reform also distrusted the "apolitical" Germans.

Science and Russian Liberalism: Alexander Herzen

Russian liberals, like liberals elsewhere in nineteenth-century Europe and the U.S., put great faith in the development of science. The liberal leader Alexander Herzen (1812–1870) was particularly interested in science. Although not a scientist himself, he followed developments in science and published a work on the history and philosophy of science, *Letters on the Study of Nature*. Herzen believed that much of the backwardness of Russian society as compared to Western Europe could be traced to the fact that Russians had failed to make Western science part of their own culture, instead being content to import science and scientists from the West, and Russian acceptance of this dependence on other countries was an aspect of the Russian inability to carry out sustained intellectual efforts.

Herzen further believed that the popularization of science would help lead to the enlightenment of Russia, and he found "apolitical" scientists who refused to engage with the public, a phenomenon he associated with Germany, to be failing in their duties to society. Science provided the mental training necessary to function in the world as citizens, a trait he found lacking in the Russian educated classes.

Herzen's ideas contributed to the liberalization of Russian society and the expansion of Russian science after the death of the repressive Tsar Nicholas I in 1855 . The prohibition on Russian students studying at foreign universities was lifted and both the Imperial Academy and Russian universities were allowed to purchase foreign books without the interference of the censors. The first Russian-language scientific periodical, the *Journal of the Imperial Academy of Sciences*, first began to appear in 1861. Late-nineteenth-century Russian scientists now fully participated in the world of Western science.

WESTERN LEARNING IN JAPAN

From 1603 to 1868, Japan was ruled by the Tokugawa shogunate, or *bakufu* (tent, or military, government). The Tokugawa family came to power after a destructive series of civil and foreign wars. The dynasty abandoned previous regimes' expansionist policies on the Asian continent, and concentrated on building a stable Japan free from civil war and foreign interference. The government of the Tokugawa shoguns was particularly concerned with the threat of Western invasion. They were aware of the Spanish conquest of the Philippines in the sixteenth century, and there was a common belief that Western conquest was aided by partisans of the Western religion, Christianity, particularly Roman Catholicism. The early seventeenth century was marked by a two-pronged response, domestic and foreign. Christianity, which had acquired a substantial Japanese following, was outlawed and crushed militarily, and the importation of Christian books banned. The last representatives of the Catholic missionary effort were expelled, killed, or tortured into converting to Buddhism. Western ships from Catholic Portugal and Spain were forbidden to trade with Japan, and Western ideas in general were initially viewed with suspicion as stalking-horses for Christianity, an idea many Western missionaries would have endorsed. Western works on science—many of them Jesuit works in Chinese that Japanese scholars would have been able to read—were destroyed or defaced to remove all mention of the Christian god.

Chinese Science in Japan

Unlike Russia, Japan possessed a scientific tradition before the arrival of Western science. This tradition, like Japanese high culture generally, had been fundamentally shaped by Japan's centuries-long contact with China. However, the differing circumstances of Japan meant that the uses it made of the sciences it imported often varied greatly from China's. For example, the Japanese calendar was a lunisolar calendar closely modeled on the Chinese calendar of the Tang dynasty. However, Japanese political authority did not rest on a "Mandate of Heaven," and Japanese rulers, unlike Chinese emperors, were not judged on their ability to produce an accurate calendar. Lacking a political incentive to keep the calendar accurate, Japanese governments let eight centuries go by without a major calendrical adjustment.

Beginning in the middle of the eighth century, Japan restricted its contacts with China and the outside world, and the lack of Japanese institutions or culture dedicated to science and mathematics led to scientific decay. Interest in science began to rise again with the reopening of cultural interchange with China in the fifteenth century following the resumption of official trade relations between Japan and China in 1401.

Japan was also a far less meritocratic society than China. Unlike the other Confucian societies of East Asia, Korea and northern Vietnam, it had no equivalent to the Chinese civil service examinations, and the political and cultural elite was far harder to get into. The principle of inheritance by birth or adoption dominated Japanese society, and there was no equivalent in Japanese popular culture to the numerous stories in Chinese literature of the poor scholar who rises to the top through talent and hard work. In brief, scholars did not have the prestige in Japan that they had in China. Instead of the learned Confucian official, the samurai warrior stood at the top of the hierarchy of careers. Learning in Japan had originally been the province of Buddhist monks, a relatively low-status group.

This situation began to change in the seventeenth century, as the Tokugawa shoguns avidly promoted classical Chinese culture. An interest in Chinese thought was now one aspect of the cultivated ideal in Tokugawa Japan. The government encouraged the import of thousands of Chinese books as long as they were free of any taint of Christianity. In addition to promoting Confucianism (or, more correctly, Neo-Confucianism) as a philosophy of loyalty to central institutions, the regime worked to create a new, less militaristic culture for Japan's dominant samurai class. The Tokugawa encouraged the samurai—about six percent of the population—to acquire basic Confucian knowledge and fostered the development of a secular elite of Confucian scholars, usually of samurai background. Given the Tokugawa lack of interest in foreign war and the domestic peace the dynasty maintained, the career of a warrior was less satisfying. The low level of institutional violence in the Tokugawa era helped drive many samurai in the direction of scholarship. However, learning, like other professions in Japan's feudal society, tended to become the hereditary property of a few families. The widespread custom of adoption helped intellectual dynasties avoid collapse when sons were not suited for the profession.

The most important scientific event in the first Tokugawa century was the state-sponsored creation of Japan's first new calendar in over 800 years, and the first calendar to be devised in Japan by Japanese rather than being taken directly from China. The intellectual leader in this effort was Shibukawa Harumi (1639–1715), originally from a family of masters of the game of go attached to the shogun's court. Such was the success of Harumi's calendar that he was made the first head of a new bureau of astronomy, which lasted for the remainder of the Tokugawa period and eventually adopted some Western techniques. As was the Japanese practice, the office of head of this bureau was made hereditary.

The Early History of Western Science in Japan

Since Japan's early cultural contacts had been almost exclusively with China and Korea, its medieval intelligentsia, unlike its Chinese contemporaries, was almost completely unfamiliar with learned traditions outside the East Asian cultural sphere. The arrival of Jesuit missionaries in the sixteenth century changed that. However, sixteenth-century Japanese leaders had been more interested in Western technology (especially guns) than in Western science. Although the Japanese became adept enough at manufacture to export guns to other Asian nations, they did not take up the science associated with Western culture at this time. Unlike in China, science played relatively little role in the Jesuit mission to Japan, and the Jesuits themselves, restricted to the port cities of the south such as Nagasaki, had little impact on the centers of Japanese intellectual life at Kyoto and political life at Edo (Tokyo).

There was, however, at least one Westerner who spread Western science after the closure of the country. During the crackdown on Christianity in Japan, an Italian Jesuit, Christovao Ferreira, (1580–1650) had been forcibly converted to Buddhism under torture. He wrote an introduction to Western cosmography, specifically that of Ptolemy and Aristotle, for the Japanese, and the work was circulated with a commentary by a Confucian scholar. However, Ferreira's treatise attracted little attention at the time. Serious Japanese interest in Western science began only in the late seventeenth century, in the seclusion era, and was less shaped by direct contact with Westerners than it was with Chinese texts.

Whereas for Peter the Great, the introduction of Western science was part of a larger project of cultural transformation, for the

Japanese rulers, Western science was only acceptable if it did not lead to cultural transformation. The prohibition on Christianity remained in force throughout the Tokugawa Era, and Japanese studying Western knowledge were quick to disavow, in most cases sincerely, any interest in Western religion.

Despite their suspicion of Christianity and Western culture in general, Western science had many attractions for Japanese. As already noted, the Japanese had adopted much of their culture from China and Korea, and had little difficulty with the idea of learning from foreign cultures. Western astronomical knowledge appealed to them for the same reasons it appealed to the Chinese—the greater precision and accuracy of its predictions. However, the openings for scientific ideas to enter were narrow. Jesuit works in Chinese, which Japanese scholars could read, were barred from the country, along with other books relating to Christianity, in 1630. However, Jesuit works imported before 1630 continued to circulate, as did their ideas.

The Dutch in Tokugawa Japan

The Tokugawa rulers did not wish to totally abandon the profitable trade with the West. Instead, they restricted it to the Protestant Dutch, the preeminent trading nation of the seventeenth century.[2] The Dutch, though Christian, had no interest in making converts in Japan or conquering the country. However, the Japanese leadership was still cautious about controlling Dutch access to Japanese society. The Dutch were restricted to a single port, Nagasaki in southern Japan, and were required to live on an artificial island called Deshima built in the middle of the harbor. Deshima was about thirty-two acres and was connected to the mainland by a single stone bridge.

The contrast between eighteenth-century Russia, which recruited foreign scientists, engineers, and physicians by the thousands, and Japan, which rigidly controlled and minimized as much as possible contact with the foreigner, was extreme. For two centuries, Deshima was the only conduit of direct contact between Japan and the West, and this extended to Western science. The Dutch imported scientific and medical books, which attracted the attention of Japanese intellectuals, particularly physicians. The Western physicians attached to the settlement were men of education, and four of

---

[2]For a survey of Dutch mercantile activities in East Asia, see Glenn Ames, *The Globe Encompassed* (2007) in this Connections Series.

them, Willem Ten Rhijne (1649–1700), Engelbert Kaempfer (1651–1716), Carl Peter Thunberg (1743–1828), and Philipp Franz von Siebold (1796–1866), were significant figures in the development of Western knowledge of Japan and Japanese knowledge of the West. Some Japanese learned Dutch, and translated Western works available in Dutch into Japanese, or were trained in Western surgery by European doctors attached to the Dutch colony. Western learning in astronomy, cosmology, physics, and particularly medicine in the eighteenth century became known as *rangaku* (Dutch studies).

Particularly in the seventeenth century, however, personal contact between Dutch and Japanese was strictly limited. Even the interpreters appointed by the Tokugawa government restricted their contacts to the discussion of purely commercial affairs, fearing the danger of too close a link with any Christians in the eyes of the shogunate. One rare opportunity for face-to-face contact between Dutchmen and interested Japanese were the annual visits that the leaders of the Dutch colony, accompanied by their physicians and others, made to pay tribute to the shogun. While the Dutch were in the shogun's capital of Edo, it was possible for Japanese to obtain a permit to visit them and converse through an interpreter.

Rangaku

Like Russians, the Japanese were usually interested in the practical applications of science rather than theoretical speculations. The closing of the country also altered the Japanese need for science. As Japanese ships no longer sailed the high seas, navigation, a powerful stimulus to research in astronomy for the West and Russia, was of no interest to Japan. Nor were the needs of the military, which shunned contact with foreign enemies and oversaw a generally peaceful internal order after the 1630s. Japanese military forces had actually regressed technologically from the gun to the sword in the seventeenth century, and there was no drive for technical improvement until the nineteenth century. Consequently, eighteenth-century Japanese interest in *rangaku* was greatest in the areas of medicine and astronomy, which was treated as an aid to calendar-making and mapping.

The first science to be transmitted via Deshima was surgery. Japanese interest in Western surgical techniques went back to the period of the Catholic mission in Japan, when a few Japanese physicians were trained in what they called "Southern barbarian surgery." Surgery, in

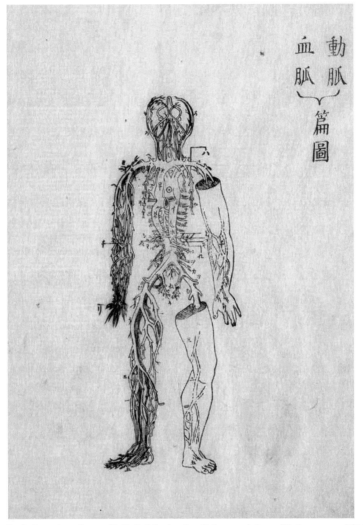

血脈　動脈
〳篇圖

Anatomical drawing from *Kaitai shinsho,* by Johann Adam Kulmus, published in Tokyo in 1774. *Courtesy National Library of Medicine*

which traditional Chinese medicine had little interest, was one of the few branches of Western scientific knowledge in Japan to survive the expulsion of the missionaries and the closing of the country. The Dutch physicians assigned to Deshima continued to teach Western surgery to interested Japanese, although this activity was illegal. In the seventeenth century, Western surgery was principally learned as a body of techniques, with little interest in Western theoretical anatomy. Some of the so-called *Komo* surgeons[3] became quite successful and were even appointed to the households of Japanese noblemen or the shogun himself.

The transmission of medical knowledge via Deshima was not a one-way project. Dutch medical men were also interested in East Asian medical techniques. In addition to tutoring interested Japanese physicians in Dutch medicine, Ten Rhijne learned of the East Asian practices of moxibustion[4] and acupuncture. On his return to Europe, he published a book on the subject of acupuncture and East Asian medicine that was widely translated and reviewed.

While the adoption of Western medicine was frequently the result of individual initiative, the adoption of Western astronomy and cosmology was driven by the needs of the central government. By the early eighteenth century, the intense fear of Christianity had dissipated among the Japanese elite (although it remained illegal), and an official opening to Western learning became possible. The Tokugawa shogun Yoshimune (reign 1716–1745) was principally interested in using Western astronomical learning for devising a more accurate calendar. Advised by the samurai astronomer Nakane Genkei (1661?–1733), Yoshimune relaxed the government ban on imported Western books in 1720. The lifting of the ban was not publicly announced because it was not meant to apply to the public. Instead, shogunate officials and a few trusted scholars would work with Western materials, while the general public was protected from anything they contained that was culturally dangerous. The lifting of the ban did not immediately result in an improved calendar. The next Japanese calendar, prepared in 1754, continued to rely on traditional Chinese methods. However, the ban was not reinstated, and the possibility of openly studying Western texts now existed. Eventually, the calendar reform of 1797 blended Western elements into an overall Chinese framework. Due to the control of astronomy by the government, however, the use of Western learning by astronomers had little influence in Japanese intellectual life in general.

Medicine would have more impact. In 1740, Yoshimune commissioned two scholars to make a study of Dutch medical works. This project initially had little influence on Japanese medicine, but one scholar, the Confucian Aoki Konyo (1698–1769), produced the first

---

[3]Japanese surgeons who trained in "surgery of the red-haired" (*komo-ryu geka*), namely surgery as taught by the Dutch.

[4]Application of the heated, and often burned, mugwort herb on the skin.

Japanese dictionary of the Dutch language. Although the shogunate government after Yoshimune's retirement in 1745 was suspicious of Western learning, by the early nineteenth century the country boasted several *Rangakujuku*, private academies for the study of the Dutch language and Western learning. Western scientific novelties, like the Leiden jar, a primitive electrical condenser that gave severe shocks, also reached Japan through Deshima.

The Japanese medical profession was particularly open to new ideas. Unlike other intellectual professions, such as Confucian scholarship or astronomy, physicians lacked strict state supervision, a governing body, or common educational institutions. Although the family of physicians to the shogun enjoyed a certain primacy, they were unable to exert authority over other physicians, many of whom worked for feudal lords outside the shogun's domains. In contrast to the small numbers of families of hereditary astronomers, there were tens of thousands of physicians scattered throughout Japan. Medicine also lacked the closed culture of many Japanese professions, which treated knowledge as secret and proprietary, handed down from teacher to student or father to son rather than openly discussed. There was a strong market for medical books, and many physicians published works aimed at a broad literate audience. There was no medical orthodoxy to be enforced, and medical practitioners had discretion in choosing between systems of Chinese and Western medicine. The so-called *Koiho* physicians rejected the elaborate structures of contemporary Chinese medicine in favor of a return to the ancient Chinese classics, and often accompanied their textual medicine with a strong dose of empiricism.

Interest in the theoretical claims of Dutch medicine grew among a circle of physicians, including Konyo's student Maeno Ryotaku (1723–1803), who were impressed by Western anatomy. Japanese physicians led by the *Koiho* School were becoming more interested in dissection at this time. Chinese medicine associated the health of the body with the flow of a life-force substance called *qi*, rather than the condition of the organs. Japanese physicians interested in the function of the organs found that Western texts seemed to give a much more accurate picture of the human body than the Chinese medical canon. Ryotaku and his associates spent great labor to produce an illustrated translation of a Dutch translation of Johann Adam Kulmus's (1689–1745) textbook *Anatomical Tables*. Their work was published in 1774 as the *New Anatomical Text*. This provoked tremendous excitement among Japanese physicians and led to the creation of a new medical tradition, "Dutch medicine," to compete with the existing schools based on Chinese medicine. Several other Dutch works in different branches of medicine were also translated. The translations improved in quality and detail—in 1808 the first Japanese anatomical texts with illustrations in copperplate rather than woodblock appeared, a change that permitted the display of much more accurate detail. By the middle of the nineteenth century, "Dutch medicine" had spread beyond its original adopters into circles of physicians in the Japanese provinces.

Not all Japanese physicians who investigated the Dutch works found them to be of value, and some denied the usefulness of dissection by reasserting the traditional Chinese medical concept of *qi*. Since a dead body is devoid of *qi* flows, they asserted, little that is relevant to health could be learned from studying it. Other physicians, known as the "eclectic" school, drew on both Western and traditional Chinese medicine. The remarkable eclectic physician Hanaoka Seishu (1760–1835) was the first physician anywhere to perform an advanced operation under general anesthesia when he removed a breast cancer in 1805.

The other scientific field in which physicians played a preponderant role, besides medicine itself, was botany. As in other medical fields, medical botany was dominated by Chinese treatises. However, just as ancient Greek and Roman works omitted many plants found in northern Europe, so Chinese works omitted many Japanese plants. Rising interest in Japanese botany among physicians led to interest in Western botany as well. Some physicians were also involved in astronomy, although this field was dominated by samurai in the eighteenth and nineteenth centuries. Most Japanese astronomers found the main value of Western works in their practical techniques for astronomical calculation, but some were interested in deeper questions of cosmology and physics. Consequently, the Japanese translated Dutch works relating to Copernican astronomy and Newtonian physics. Inevitably, Japanese translators of these Western scientific works, like their Russian contemporaries, faced the problem of vocabulary. The works abounded with words for which there was no precise Japanese equivalent. Unlike the Russian translation effort, which was centralized and state-directed, Japanese translators were on their own in either adapting Western words to Japanese or finding Japanese words with a similar meaning that could be put in their place. The Japanese also adopted some Western astronomical technology, notably the telescope. By the early nineteenth century, Japanese-made telescopes were widely used among astronomers.

Western Science, Chinese Learning, and Japanese Nativism

Chinese learning in Japan, as in China, was not a monolith, and from the reopening to China in the seventeenth century, differing schools of Chinese thought had been represented in Japan. Although the thirteenth-century Zhu Xi school of Neo-Confucianism had received the backing of the shogunate, other schools flourished in private academies and among individual scholars. *Rangaku* studies benefited from the intellectual pluralism of eighteenth-century Japan, where the Zhu Xi School was under increasing attack. Zhu Xi's concept of an all-embracing synthesis of knowledge of the heavens, Earth, and humanity was rejected even by some Zhu Xi scholars, and the possibility of admitting the importance of specialized Western knowledge in particular fields was opened.

One reason for interest in *rangaku* was an eighteenth-century Japanese cultural reaction against the historical dominance of Chinese thought. Many Japanese intellectuals sought to return to indigenous traditions, such as the Shinto religion and reverence for the emperor, in opposition to Buddhism and Confucianism, both of which had reached Japan from China and Korea. These intellectuals became known as the champions of *kokugaku* (national learning) and asserted Japan's superiority to other cultures. Although Western thought was not Japanese, it also was not Chinese, and many *kokugaku* intellectuals were attracted to what could be presented as *rangaku*'s superiority to Chinese thought in some areas and its usefulness at promoting Japan's emergence from the giant shadow cast by China in East Asian culture. The influential *kokugaku* teacher Hirata Atsutane (1776–1843) claimed that Copernican astronomy, putting the Sun at the center of the universe, endorsed the Japanese Shinto practice of worshipping the Sun Goddess Amaterasu. Atsutane's Shintoism had strong monotheistic elements, and he praised Western scientists for their acknowledgement of a creator God. He also attempted to naturalize foreign medical knowledge by claiming that both Chinese and Western medicine were originally Japanese, the gift of the Japanese gods.

The Turn against Western Science

By the early nineteenth century Japan was under increasing pressure from the new imperial powers of the West. Despite the desire of the shogun's government to maintain the "closed country" policy, educated Japanese were becoming aware of the power of the Western nations. The old system, whereby the Japanese basically controlled the terms of trade with the Dutch, was now threatened by new and aggressive powers—Britain, Russia, and the United States—who threatened to overpower Japan and bend it to their will. Some believed that reform of the country, including the government, was necessary for the nation to retain its freedom of action. Reformers such as Honda Toshiaki (1744–1821) argued for the adoption of Western science, which they claimed was the world's most advanced, as part of a broad program for a more open and assertive Japan that would follow Western rather than Chinese models. In this politically charged atmosphere, the study of Western knowledge, including Western science, took on a political quality both the government and its opponents were aware of.

The Tokugawa regime had a paradoxical relationship to Western science. Knowledge of Western science and technology could be useful if a struggle with Western powers was inevitable, but excessive interest in Western science by the Japanese (and Western science was the most prominent representative of Western culture in Japan) could lead to interest in Western customs and politics and discontent with the conservative Tokugawa social and political order.

The reforming eighteenth-century Confucian minister Matsudaira Sadanobu (1759–1829) was the first Japanese official to formulate a policy for Western books. Sadanobu believed in a strongly regulated intellectual life in opposition to what he viewed as the laxity that had overcome Japan in recent decades. Under his leadership, the *bakufu*, which in the eighteenth century had showed little concern for controversies within Confucianism, strongly endorsed the Neo-Confucianism of the Zhu Xi School and forbade other interpretations as heretical. Sadanobu further believed that Western books were useful in the fields of astronomy, geography, and medicine, but their too free circulation was dangerous, encouraging idle speculation and subversive ideas. Consequently, Sadanobu set up a system whereby the Japanese government collected Western books at Nagasaki to control their distribution. Only *bakufu*-approved scholars would now have access to the new learning of the West. The arrival of Western knowledge was also slowed by the decay of trade between the Netherlands and Japan. Japan's growing economy had less need for Dutch goods, and the trade was no longer a great source of profit for the Dutch.

The early nineteenth century saw further efforts to centralize Western knowledge for the government's benefit. The usefulness of Western learning became apparent with the calendar reform of 1798, and in 1811 the shogunate opened an Office for the Translation of Barbarian Writing to promote *rangaku*, expanding beyond the fields of astronomy and medicine. The government sought to use this new bureaucracy not only to promote Western learning, but also to control its distribution by taking it from private hands. The *bakufu* continued to use Western learning, as in the excellent series of maps of Japan produced by the great cartographer Ino Tadakata (1745–1818), who used a Western-derived latitude system.

Siebold and the Crackdown on Independent Rangaku Scholars

By the 1820s, Japan was under even more pressure from European powers and the United States to open the country to trade. Some Japanese leaders responded with an increased hostility to things foreign, a hostility directed not primarily against China but against the West. This included *rangaku*.

The arrival of the German physician Philipp Franz Balthasar von Siebold at Deshima in 1823 led to the crisis of Western learning in Tokugawa Japan. Siebold brought to the community of students of "Dutch learning" the personal influence and missionary zeal of a Western-trained scientist, bringing Western learning to Japan far more actively and systematically than previous Nagasaki physicians. Siebold gathered a large group of Japanese students and lectured on clinical procedures, as well as zoology and botany. He also set his pupils to writing essays in the Western scientific tradition on issues in Japanese medicine and natural history. Siebold's connections with Japanese scientists led to disaster when the government astronomer Takahashi Kageyasu (1785–1829) showed him some of Tadataka's survey maps of Japan in exchange for Western charts of Sakhalin Island north of Japan. When the government learned of this it was quite upset, as accurate maps had obvious military uses. Siebold was expelled from Japan as a spy in 1829, and his students were imprisoned. Takahashi was imprisoned and died shortly thereafter, and many of his pupils and associates were also imprisoned. A later persecution, the *bansha no goku* (imprisonment of barbarian associates) of 1839, led to the death or imprisonment of several Western-influenced scientists, including the leading *rangaku* physician Takano Choei (1804–1850).

The political crackdown was accompanied by a more active censorship and moves against Western ideas. In 1849, Chinese-style physicians in the shogunal territories succeeded in getting a ban on Western medicine, except for the fields of surgery and ophthalmology. The following year all circulation to the Japanese public of translations of Western books was forbidden.

The reaction against Western learning, though, did not mean that the government did not continue to recognize its usefulness in some areas. The last calendrical reform the Tokugawa government produced, the *Tenporeki* of 1842, was also the first based entirely on Western astronomy.

The Japanese Crisis of the Mid-Nineteenth Century and Western Learning

The Japanese policy of isolation was increasingly untenable given the power and aggressiveness of the Western nations in East Asia. A particular dividing line was the First Opium War between Great Britain and China from 1839 to 1842. Many Japanese still saw China as the center of civilization, and its humiliating defeat attracted great interest and apprehension. Many Japanese intellectuals and government officials feared, moreover, that their own country would be next without strong reforms. China's defeat was also a setback for the prestige of Confucianism and Chinese learning generally in Japan. Japanese fears were accentuated by the visit to Japan of the American Commodore Matthew C. Perry (1794–1858) and his fleet in 1854. The fact that the Japanese government was unable to deny Perry access to Japanese ports meant the policy of seclusion was untenable, and a technologically backward Japan could be subject to the same creeping loss of sovereignty currently being suffered by China.

Western science was an important part of the Tokugawa response, but it was still contested. There was an attempt by conservative shogunate officials to separate the teaching of technology—necessary for military purposes—from Western science, which could lead to dangerous views threatening Japan's stability. However, by the 1860s, the government had begun to gingerly sponsor study abroad for young Japanese military officers—a shogunate naval officer went to the University of Leiden in 1862 . The domain of Choshu in the south—a leader in contact with Westerners—sent a student to the University of London two years later. The pieces were moving into place for the far more complete Japanese adoption of Western science following the over-throw of the Tokugawas in the Meiji Restoration of 1867.

SOURCES

■ Jakob Staehlin von Storcksberg, Founding the Imperial Academy of Sciences of St. Petersburg

Jakob Staehlin von Storcksberg was one of the many Germans who made their way to Russia in the eighteenth century. A member of the Imperial Academy of Sciences of St. Petersburg, Staehlin was ac-quainted with old Russian courtiers who had grown up at Peter's court. His *Original Anecdotes of Peter the Great*, while not denying the monarch's brutality, was concerned with portraying the Tsar as a great Russian hero and modernizer. The following anecdote recounts the founding of the Academy.

How does Staehlin describe the recruitment process? How do Peter and the unnamed privy counselor see the impact of the new in-stitution on Russia? How does Staehlin use the founding of the Academy to serve his overall project of depicting Peter as a wise "en-lightened monarch"?

The Tsar, wishing to execute the project he had long formed, of found-ing an academy in his new city, gave orders to his ambassadors abroad to send him an account of all the learned men of eminence in the places where they resided, that he might make a choice of such as it was nec-essary to invite to Russia, to form the society he had in view. He even wrote to some of them in his own hand, to recommend this affair to their attention.

The conversation turning one day on this subject at the Emperor's table—"Such an establishment as Your Majesty is speaking of" said a privy counsellor "would certainly be of great utility to the state; but I doubt whether the nation at large would derive much advantage from a society composed entirely of learned men of the first order, who would pay little or no attention to the instruction of youth."

"Why not?" replied the Tsar. "I have my views in what I will do, and will explain them to you. These learned men will write books treat-ing of the elements of the different sciences, and I will direct them to be translated into our language. They will be obliged to explain them to their pupils, who, in their turn, will explain them to theirs. Works of other kinds, though written in Latin, will do us honour throughout Europe. The world will see that we cultivate the sciences, instead of despising them like barbarians; and all the officers of my empire, whether of the different boards, the chancery, or treasury, will consult the academy in all difficult cases."

Jakob Staehlin von Storcksberg, *Original Anecdotes of Peter the Great* (London, 1788), 343–344.

■ Ekaterina Dashkova and the Reform of the Russian Academy

In 1782, Tsarina Catherine II the Great appointed Ekaterina Dashkova director of the Imperial Academy of Sciences of St. Petersburg, the only woman to head a Scientific Academy before the twentieth century. In this passage in Dashkova's memoirs, she discusses her first meeting with the Academicians, and how she tried to deal with them. What does Dashkova sees as the main problems with the Academy? How does she attempt to resolve them? Why would Russia, unlike the more "progressive" countries of the West, have a woman director of its Academy?

As soon as I entered the hall of their sittings, addressing the professors and members there assembled, I lamented my own deficiency in scientific attainments, but spoke of the high respect I entertained for science, of which M. Euler's[5] presence amongst them, whose auspices I had solicited in conducting me to the academy, would, I hoped, be received as the most solemn pledge I could offer.

After having delivered these few words I took my seat, and remarked that M. Schteline, professor of Allegory, as he was called, had taken his place next to the director's chair. This gentleman, whose pretensions to science might, perhaps, be suited to the designation he bore, gained this extraordinary title and appointment in the time of Peter the Third [reign 1762], and with it the rank of councillor of state, which, answering to that of major-general, gave him, as he thought, a claim to the highest distinction amongst the members of the academy. Turning, therefore, to M. Euler, "Sit down, Sir," I said, "wherever you please, and whatever seat you may happen to take, that seat must consequently be deemed the highest."

---

[5]Leonhart Euler, Swiss mathematician and long-term member of the academy.

The lively feeling of delight and approbation excited by this un-premeditated tribute of respect to his talents was not confined to the son-in-law and grandson; there was not a professor present (with the exception of the professor of Allegory) who did not sympathize in their feelings, and with tears in his eyes acknowledge the merits and superiority of this venerable character.

From the hall of assembly I passed on into the chancery, where a registry is kept of everything relative to the pecuniary and economical concerns of the establishment. Here the superintendents were at their posts, to whom I observed, that a general idea had gone abroad of the great neglect and malversation[6] which had been suffered under the late director, such as not only to have exhausted the revenue of the academy, but to have left it in debt.

"Henceforward," I said, "it must be our common duty to redress these abuses; and as it is not necessary that any branch of the establishment should fall to decay, the most obvious and efficacious means in our power are, to apply exclusively to its own wants and advantages all the resources which the academy may possess. With this view, therefore, I am resolved neither to enrich myself at its expense, nor to allow the smallest peculation in any of the subordinate offices; and could I but persuade every one to regulate his conduct strictly by this principle, I should very soon be in a situation to recompense the zealous and deserving, by promotion or some addition to their salaries."

The *Commentaries* which had formerly been published by the academy, in two volumes quarto,[7] yearly, had dwindled down into one, and were now discontinued altogether for want of the requisite types. The printing office and presses I found in the utmost disorder, and in want of everything to make the latter effective. It was one of my first cares to have them completely repaired, and to have such types provided as were fit and appropriate; and it was not long before two volumes of *Commentaries* were again issued from the academy, compiled, for the most part, from articles which had been furnished by M. Euler.

Ekaterina Dashkova, *Memoirs of the Princess Daschkaw, Lady of Honour to Catherine II*, trans. W. Bradford, Two volumes (London: Henry Colburn, 1840), I, 302–305.

■ Honda Toshiaki on Western Science and Political Reform

Japanese reformer Honda Toshiaki was concerned by both Russian expansion north of Japan and the general backwardness of Japan

---

[6]Misconduct in a public office.
[7]A volume that is roughly 9 by 12 inches.

compared to European civilization Toshiaki idealized without any firsthand experience of it. His solution was for Japan to adopt an aggressive policy of economic expansion and colonization, with Western science playing an important role. This excerpt from his *A Secret Plan of Government* praises the pragmatic value of Western science. How does Toshiaki relate Western knowledge to imperialism? How accurate is his knowledge of Western science? How does he view the history of the West relative to China and Japan?

At this point we must discuss the foundations of colonization—the sciences of astronomy and mathematics. In Japan these sciences are not as yet fully known, and there are few men who understand their significance. Even in China the principles of astronomy and mathematics have roughly been understood since the arrival of a number of Europeans late in the seventeenth century. If, in connection with colonization projects, ships cross the seas without reference to the principles of astronomy and mathematics, there is no way to tell how much easier sea travel is than land travel. The name of the book in which the natural laws behind these principles are contained is *Schatkamer*, a European work. One may learn from the latitude of a particular island what its climate is like throughout the year, and without actually visiting an island, one can predict in this way whether it will prove fertile. This may be done with certainty, false tales need not be believed.

Excerpt from *The Japanese Discovery of Europe, 1720–1830*, Revised Edition, by Donald Keene, 171. Copyright © 1952 and 1969 by Donald Keene. All rights reserved. Used with the permission of Stanford University Press, www.sup.org

■ Late Tokugawa Science in Western Eyes

Curiosity about the remote, closed society of Japan was growing in mid-nineteenth century Europe. One compilation of Dutch writings on Japan in English translation, drawing heavily on Philipp Von Siebold, was the anonymous *Japan and the Japanese in the Nineteenth Century* (1852). The following excerpt, probably taken from Siebold's account, describes Japanese science.

How does the Western author evaluate Japanese science? How does he distinguish between Japanese and Chinese science? How does this passage display both the confidence of nineteenth-century Western science and a sense of unease?

The only sciences that can be said to be cultivated in Japan, are medicine and astronomy, and upon these we are assured that original works, as well as translations of all European publications, accessible to the Japanese through Dutch versions, are constantly appearing. Of the merits of the original works we have no means of judging, save by inference from the reports of the abilities and knowledge of the Japanese physicians and astronomers; and on this head, those of the medical travellers are favourable. Dr. von Siebold dwells eulogistically upon the zeal with which physicians from all parts of the empire thronged about him to acquire medical science of a higher character than their own; and his opinion of the intelligence and knowledge evinced by their questions has been already mentioned. The latter remark applies equally to the astronomers; and it may be added, that their sense of the scientific superiority of Europe, alone, places the Japanese far above the self-sufficient Chinese.

Of the proficiency of the medical profession in Japan, some further notion may be formed from the assertion that acupuncture and moxa-burning are native inventions. The former of these remedies, having been introduced into this country, needs no description; but it may be worth mentioning, that among the books brought to Europe by Heer Titsingh,[8] is one containing accurate directions for its use, with an enumeration of the maladies it is calculated to relieve, and accompanied by a doll, upon which is marked every part of the frame adapted to the operation, according to the several cases. Mora-burning is a means of blistering, or making an issue, by burning balls of fungus (moxa) upon the skin.[9]

The drugs employed in Japanese pharmacy are mostly animal and vegetable, chemistry being far too superficially and imperfectly known to allow physicians to venture upon mineral remedies. But botany, as connected with the knowledge of simples,[10] is diligently cultivated, and the medicines used are said to be generally beneficial; the chief reliance, however, is upon diet, acupuncture, and the moxa. Superstition is the main obstacle to the progress of medicine and surgery: its baneful influence was apparent in what has been incidentally mentioned respecting the obstetric department of the science; and the pollution incurred by contact with death, renders dissection, and consequently anatomical science, impossible.

---

[8]Isaac Titsingh (1745–1812), a Dutch surgeon, merchant, and ambassador of the Dutch East India Company (VOC) to the court of the shogun.

[9]See also note 6, above.

[10]Single plants. In pharmacological terms, a "simple" is an uncompounded medicament consisting of a single ingredient.

In astronomy, the proficiency made is yet greater, perhaps, from there being no superstitious impediments in the way of progress in the science. The Japanese astronomers study the most profound works, such as Lalande's treatises,[11] that have been translated into Dutch, and have learned the use of most European instruments. These they have taught Japanese artists to imitate, and Meylan[12] saw good telescopes, barometers, and thermometers, of Japanese workmanship. In consequence, the almanacks, which were formerly imported from China, are now constructed at home, the calculation of eclipses included, in the Yedo[13] and Dairi[14] colleges.

Philipp Franz von Siebold, *Japan and the Japanese in the Nineteenth Century* (London: John Murray, 1852), 307–309.

---

[11]The French astronomer Joseph Jérome Lefrançais de Lalande (1732–1807).
[12]Germain Felix Meylan (1785–1831), director of the VOC factory at Deshima from 1826 to 1830. He authored *Sketches of the Manners and Usages of Japan* (1830).
[13]Edo, present-day Tokyo, the shogunate capital.
[14]The imperial court in Kyoto.

CHAPTER

4

Africa in the Age of Imperialism and Nationalism, 1860–1960

The nineteenth and early twentieth centuries are often referred to as the "Age of Imperialism." In this period, European countries, led by Britain and France, exploited their military, technological, and economic superiority over non-Western peoples to build the largest colonial empires the world had ever seen. Science played a central role in the *Imperial Project*.

Africa is the world's second largest continent after Asia, home to a diverse range of environments and societies. European powers had a long history in Africa. North Africa and Egypt had been part of the Roman Empire, and medieval Europeans had traded with North and West Africans. The Portuguese voyages of the fifteenth century also initiated a process whereby Europeans began to establish fortresses along the west and east African coasts to carry on the transatlantic slave trade, as well as other commerce with African peoples. However, despite these incursions, African states and peoples had mostly retained their independence through the mid-nineteenth century. But when European empire-builders finally arrived in Africa, nowhere was their advance more rapid. The late nineteenth century saw the "Scramble for Africa," a frenzy of colonial activity. In a few decades, a handful of European powers established control over nearly the entire continent, leaving only the small independent states of Liberia and Ethiopia. Britain and France were particularly acquisitive and successful, but they were joined by Germany, Spain, Portugal, Italy, and Belgium.

The late nineteenth century was also a period of dramatic developments in science. Charles Darwin (1809–1882) put forth his theory of evolution in *Origin of Species* (1859). Darwin's theory of evolution through natural selection, itself derived from a mass of natural historical data from all over the world, provided a new organizing principle for the life sciences. Shortly afterward, the theory of the gene also vastly altered biology. The physical sciences were breaking into new areas of field theory, electromagnetic theory, and eventually the beginnings of quantum mechanics. The role of science and scientists in society was changing too. (The English word "scientist" was first used in 1834.) The population of scientists was growing, while scientific institutions and disciplines were multiplying at a phenomenal speed and were ever more closely integrated with governments. A broad public took interest in scientific issues, buying and reading science books and journals, attending lectures, and visiting museums, gardens, and zoos.

Imperialism and science were deeply intertwined. The quest for empire was often viewed as a quest for knowledge. Africa in the nineteenth century was frequently referred to by Europeans and white Americans as the "Dark Continent." The image of darkness contained many meanings, but one of them was the darkness of ignorance. European explorers and scientists, such as the Englishman Richard Francis Burton or the German Karl Peters saw part of their mission as illuminating the Dark Continent by making it the subject of European knowledge. The fundamental asymmetries of the imperial power relationship were reflected in the epistemology of imperial science. Europeans and their colonial descendants were "knowers," the native peoples, animals and plants of their empires were "the known." But scientists in the colonial world were not merely seekers of knowledge. They could also wield power to a far greater degree than they could in Europe. Scientists in Europe were limited by the vested interests of established classes and institutions, and the voice of organized science was only one among a number filling the public square. In the colonial world, authoritarian governing structures led to a more authoritarian science, as scientists working with colonial governments were often able to disregard the wishes and institutional structures of indigenous societies.

Western science was not merely imposed on African reality. New sciences, such as tropical medicine and "ethnopsychiatry," were also born out of the colonial encounter.

EXPLORATION

Exploration of the African interior was the culmination of a process that had begun with the voyages of Columbus and Vasco da Gama in the fifteenth century—the project of making the world known to European science. However, Africa was in a better position during the early modern period to resist European penetration than were North and South America. For one thing, it had a unique and pervasive set of diseases. Over the millennia, indigenous Africans had acquired the adaptations and immunities that enabled them to live in Africa's tough disease environments, but African diseases remained extremely dangerous to those who had not grown up in Africa. African societies, although usually perfectly willing to trade with Europeans and other outsiders, were also more able to defend themselves militarily against invasion than Native American or indigenous Australian societies. The Africans Europeans came into contact with along the coast were unwilling to allow Europeans to venture into the interior.

Geography was particularly bound up with conquest. In the beginning of the nineteenth century, much of Africa was "Darkest Africa," the proverbial blank space on the map. The sources of its major rivers and the geography of its interior were virtually unknown. Even in the eighteenth century, when the South Seas, Australia, and the interior of America were being explored and mapped to an unprecedented degree, most of Africa remained closed. As America had been during the European conquests, Africa was mapped and measured by its new invaders in the nineteenth century. However, cartography and geodesy had advanced greatly since the days of the conquistadors. The scientifically qualified explorer or expedition had advanced knowledge of astronomy, trigonometry, and cartography to accurately map the newly "discovered" lands. In turn, the maps and other geographical information the explorers generated could be used by armed expeditions of conquest.

Exploration was often sponsored by governments or quasi-governmental organizations. Britain's Royal Geographical Society had begun as the Association for Promoting the Discovery of the Inland Districts of Africa, the sponsor of some of the earliest European explorations of the African interior. Scientific groups not only enabled imperial conquests, sometimes they actually lobbied for them. Groups dedicated to geography were a natural place for colonial expansionists to congregate, given the connection between mapping a region and claiming it. In France, the scramble for Africa was marked by the foundation of provincial geographical societies with explicitly economic goals, which sponsored expeditions with practical aims, such as mapping the best route for a trans-Saharan railway route tying together the French possessions in West and Central Africa.

In addition to geography and cartography, natural history was another scientific discipline wrapped up in exploration. The tropical zone in particular was full of plants and animals previously unknown to European biologists. Explorers were expected to make large collections of specimens, and frequently drew on the knowledge of indigenous Africans, not always with acknowledgement. However, in order for a plant or animal to be truly "known" by European scientists, neither indigenous knowledge nor the descriptions of explorers were adequate. Ideally, a live specimen needed to reach a European botanical garden or menagerie, where it could be assigned a "scientific name" and a place in botanical or zoological classification. The great collecting institutions of Europe—the Royal Botanical Gardens at Kew, the Museum of Natural History with its associated gardens in Paris—conceived of themselves as living libraries of natural history.

CONQUEST

Exploration was only a first step in the road to *Empire*. The "Scramble for Africa" was an effort to convert the hard-won European knowledge of Africa into effective control. Each European competitor had not only to overcome the resistance of indigenous Africans and the African environment, but also deal with its colonial rivals. The competitive drive to lay claim to territories before rivals is one reason why the continent was partitioned at a speed unrivalled in the history of empire-building. In this contest, mapping and describing a territory helped establish the legitimacy of a claim to rule it.

Although by the nineteenth century European military and economic power far exceeded anything indigenous African societies could muster, disease remained among the biggest challenges to would-be empire builders. Tropical Africa acquired a legendary reputation as a killer, the "white man's graveyard." Africa, outside the far north and south and a few other highland areas, was considered an undesirable posting. Africans themselves were also made more vulnerable to disease by European imperialism's disruption of local communities and the microorganisms that expeditions carried with them from one part of Africa to another. African immunity was not a continent-wide equilibrium, but a series of adaptations to local disease environments that could be easily disrupted. The relocation of Africans by imperialism made them more vulnerable to disease, although this concern was much less important to Europeans than their own vulnerability.

Western medicine itself was undergoing rapid transformations in the era, many connected to the epidemic diseases in Europe itself, the result of the industrial revolution, and the rapid creation of large cities with poor sanitation and overcrowded housing that followed. The most important development in medical science in the late nineteenth century was the creation of bacteriological medicine, which identified epidemic diseases with specific microorganisms—the "germ theory of disease."

The scramble for Africa occurred at the same time that the germ theory of disease was rapidly making medicine a far more scientific discipline. The study of disease became less oriented to finding effective treatments on a "hit or miss" basis (as quinine had been found to be effective against malaria) and more about the identification of the specific microorganisms associated with specific illnesses. The scientific response to the dangers of African disease was the development of a new subfield, tropical medicine. African diseases presenting challenges included malaria, yellow fever, sleeping sickness, and bilharzias (also known as schistosomiasis or snail fever). Animal diseases like rinderpest, an infectious viral disease affecting cattle and domestic

Statue of Shapona, the West African God of Smallpox. *Courtesy CDC/Global health Odyssey*

buffalo, were also studied. Europeans believed that social means, such as quarantine, the relocation of African populations, or the slaughter of domestic animals believed to be carriers of infection were effective ways to combat these diseases and imposed them on the indigenous peoples. Efforts such as these, however, often only worsened the problem, as relocated populations carried their diseases with them to new territories.

EXPLOITATION

Once European control over African territories had been established, European powers wanted to know how to most efficiently exploit their newly acquired resources. Science was a tool to answer this question.

In most of the colonies, colonial powers focused their efforts on agriculture and livestock raising. This often required the disruption of local agricultural economies based on multicrop subsistence farming, in which the principal goal of crop raising was providing sufficient food and other goods for the local community. Colonial powers were more interested in agriculture that produced a profit, and often imposed or encouraged a shift toward "cash crop" monoculture, in which a given crop was raised for the purpose of being sold, often to businesses or the government based in the colonial power itself. This fitted the nineteenth-century ideology of free trade and economic specialization, which valued production for the global market over production for local needs and saw colonies as producers of raw materials for industry. The agricultural research stations established by colonial rulers focused on export crops, such as coffee, cocoa beans, or rubber, rather than the subsistence African crops, such as cassava. In the many cases where the new cash crop was one with no history in the region, shifting the agricultural economy to it required the imposition of a particular regime of knowledge, where experts from the colonial power explained and enforced the techniques for growing and harvesting the new crop.

Confident in their science, European colonial administrators often ignored or treated with contempt indigenous agricultural practices. African production methods were often categorized by colonial administrators as "laziness," the worst of sins to nineteenth-century capitalist Europeans. Colonial administrators and other Europeans were already predisposed to make this judgment due to the racist stereotypes of Africans as lazy that had developed in the slavery era.

The competition among imperial powers that continued after the partition of Africa also fostered scientific study of colonial resources. Rivalry was a particularly effective tool for colonial lobbyists attempting to get home governments to devote more money to agricultural and other economic research in Africa. British colonial administrators in the late nineteenth century looked nervously at the botanical and mineralogical studies carried out in the German

African possessions, and used the growing British-German rivalry to lobby the British government for more scientific resources.

Another aspect of the economic exploitation of colonial resources was the development of the science of acclimatization. It was hoped that economically useful plants and animals found in a particular colony could be introduced to other colonies or even to the territory of the colonial power itself. Of course, the spread of crops, within and beyond empires, has had a long history. However, nineteenth-century acclimatists hoped to make the process scientific, through applying the experimental method and applying scientific biological problems to acclimatization. France was the center of acclimatization studies. This was partly because French biologists were more receptive than German or British ones to the idea of living things adapting themselves to the environment, rather than having a nature fixed by heredity. The desire to acclimate crops led to the creation of one of the characteristic scientific institutions of colonialism—the experimental crop research garden, where different new plants were raised to test their possible usefulness.

Of course, not all research into Africa was motivated by immediately utilitarian concerns. The colonies also provided additional data for European scientific debates. One of the major questions in mid-nineteenth century botany was that of "phytogeography"—the geographical distribution of plant species and genera. Plant surveys of African territories provided fresh information relevant to such questions.

The dangers and inconveniences of the colonies, as compared with the centers of science in Europe, meant that they were most attractive to young scientists in their twenties with a reputation to make. The major centers of research into Africa, such as the Institut Louis Pasteur in France or the London School of Hygiene and Tropical Medicine, remained in Europe. Government efforts to attract older scientists to studies of colonial problems in the colonies themselves were usually failures, although occasionally an offer was generous enough to lure a big-name scientist for a temporary visit, as when the great German microbiologist Robert Koch (1843–1910), a future winner of the Nobel Prize, was brought to Africa by the British government to study a virulent plague, "Rhodesian redwater," affecting cattle in the British colony of Rhodesia (present-day Zimbabwe). Another source of older scientists, but usually not scientists of the top rank, was European militaries, which had the power to order people to Africa. As elsewhere, militaries had a great demand for physicians and cartographers.

WESTERN AND AFRICAN KNOWLEDGE IN THE FORMATION OF AFRICAN NATURAL HISTORY

One of the most striking aspects of Africa in Western eyes was the diversity of its flora and fauna. The identification and classification of species new to European knowledge was one of the principal tasks of botanists and zoologists in the nineteenth century. However, while Westerners could skillfully dissect animals and classify the parts of plants, much knowledge of animals and plants in their natural settings rested with Africans. Building the natural history of Africa required European scientists to incorporate African knowledge. (Of course, this situation was not unique to Africa, but occurred wherever Western scientists encountered indigenous peoples.) The "collecting expeditions" of Western natural history museums, botanical gardens, and zoos relied on native African guides, hunters, and bearers.

African knowledge, however, was not viewed as equal to European knowledge. In order for a piece of African knowledge to become a "scientific fact" it had to be verified or "sponsored" by a European with scientific credentials. The European might then often receive credit for the "discovery." A classic example is the okapi, a relative of the giraffe and one of the last large mammals to be "discovered" by Europeans. Native to the jungles of the Congo, the okapi was known to their Pygmy inhabitants as the o'api, but it was known only vaguely to Europeans from the Pygmies's descriptions. Europeans concluded that the unknown animal was related to the zebra and more distantly to the horse. A British colonial official, Sir Harry Johnston (1858–1927), became interested in the mysterious animal and obtained a few pieces of its skin, which he sent to the Zoological Society of London. The pygmies also showed him okapi tracks, but the tracks were cloven, so Johnston dismissed them as not real okapi tracks, since a relative of the horse and zebra would have solid hooves. Although neither Johnston nor the Zoological Society of London had ever seen a live okapi, the animal received the name *Equus Johnstoni*—"Johnston's horse."

SCIENCE AND IMPERIAL IDEOLOGY

Science also played an important role in how European nations explained and justified colonial rule. The rationality and modernity of science, viewed as an exclusively Western activity, was contrasted with the "backwardness" of traditional African societies and the "fanaticism" of Islam. This was an extension to the colonies of struggles in the home countries themselves, where science and secularism were increasingly portrayed as allies against traditionalism and superstition. This was particularly marked in the French case, where science played a central role in the "civilizing mission" French imperialists claimed their country was carrying out in its African and other colonies. The nineteenth century in France was marked by an ongoing struggle between the Catholic Church and secularists over such issues as the form government should take (monarchy or republic), foreign policy, and control of national education and curriculum. In this struggle, French secularism acquired a missionary and universalistic cast that affected colonial administration. Some of the greatest French secularizers, such as Prime Minister Jules Ferry (1832–1893), were also the strongest supporters of French colonialism. Europeans also put forth the allegedly life-saving qualities of "scientific" medicine as a justification for imperial rule.

Agricultural science played a particularly important role in justifying colonial regimes. Many Europeans and white Americans believed that those peoples who could not or did not make use of agricultural land in the most "efficient" fashion—efficiency defined by the global market—had forfeited their rights over it. By the nineteenth century, the belief in the superior European ability to use land efficiently became bound up in the belief in the superiority of European science. (Similar beliefs were held by white Americans, who believed Native Americans had forfeited their rights over land by failing to exploit it in an efficient manner.) "Natives" were ignorant as well as lazy, and it was the duty of white men to teach them more advanced agriculture. Colonial administrations justified forced agricultural change in the name of the superiority of "scientific" agriculture. ("Scientific" innovations in agriculture were not only opposed by indigenous people. In many cases, Europeans who had immigrated to the colonies to become farmers also distrusted the "scientific" schemes of central administrators and their advisors.)

This belief in science was shared by different colonial powers, and sometimes fostered cooperation across political lines to carry out scientific research. In the nineteenth century, a time of intense national rivalry, many also supported the idea that science was international. However, scientific organizations founded in colonial Africa were integrated with those of the colonizing power to create lines of authority that paralleled those of the imperial structure itself, rather than being integrated across the boundaries of European colonies. The scientific connections of French colonies in Africa were with French institutions, such as the Museum of Natural History in Paris, rather than with those of British African colonies. The research agendas of colonial institutions were usually determined by European scientists far removed from the colonies. This was particularly true of French colonies, drawing on the French tradition of administrative centralism.

"RACIAL SCIENCE" IN COLONIAL AFRICA

By the beginning of the colonial period in Africa, Europeans and other Westerners had accumulated a body of science dedicated to asserting and examining the inferiority of African and other "colored" peoples. Racist science did not originate in colonial Africa. European racism had a long history, but the most important period for its expression in scientific terms was the eighteenth century, when the slave trade was at its height and when many European and Euro-American scientists were obsessed with biological classification. Over this period, scientific justifications of slavery based on assertions of the biological inferiority of African peoples replaced religious ones. Although the scramble for Africa followed the abolition of slavery in most European countries and their colonies, and European imperialists often justified their colonial projects as opposing African slavery, they inherited, expanded, and sometimes disputed slavery's racial science.

Emerging systems of racial hierarchy invariably placed Europeans on top, and usually placed black Africans at or near the bottom, with other groups in between. Traditional European antiblack attitudes had emphasized the ugliness of blacks in European eyes and the biblical story of the curse of Ham, the son of Noah, who was supposedly the ancestor of Africans. Although these arguments continued to be made, there was a growing emphasis in European antiblack literature on blacks' alleged physical, intellectual, and moral deficiencies expressed as the assertion of scientific truth about the essential nature of black people. This played a central role in justifying the colonial project. Like colonialists elsewhere, European colonialists in Africa justified what they were doing as in the interest of the Africans themselves. Africans did not have the right to self-determination due to their racial inferiority.

Nineteenth-century scientists and imperial theorists often placed races on a developmental scale analogous to the different stages in an individual life. Africans were commonly referred to as overgrown children in need of the "adult supervision" of Europeans. The metaphor of Africans as children and Europeans as parents or older siblings was common in colonial discourse. European rule could be justified as better suited for "childlike" Africans than self-rule. However, not all scientific racists supported the colonial project. Many argued that imperial expansion would lead to the dilution of the "white race."

Racial classification was central to a new scientific discipline which emerged in the nineteenth-century physical anthropology. Physical anthropologists measured and analyzed human bodies, particularly their skeletons. They studied both living and extinct human types. Much of their effort was to identify differences between races and classify humans accordingly. Physical anthropologists often viewed individuals in terms of deviation or conformity from a "pure" racial type. The rhetoric of purity was linked to the idea of seeing deviations from the idealized racial type as "degenerate." The range of physical types found in Africa—as well as the hominid fossils to be found there—made it a tempting field of research for physical anthropologists.

A key component of the emerging concept of race was the emphasis on heredity, rather than environment, as the most important factor in shaping human beings. The idea that the different physical qualities of different peoples was a result of the different climates and environments they were exposed to was an old one. For example, African people were believed to be black because of their exposure to the heat of the tropical Sun. The African climate was blamed for African racial "inferiority." Although climactic considerations were not forgotten, European thinkers increasingly ascribed differences between human groups to inherited differences, independent of environment. The discovery of genetics in the nineteenth century and the belief that acquired characteristics could not be passed down to offspring contributed to the idea of the "fixed" inherent nature of human races. A common "biological" theory of black inferiority was that the development of black children was arrested by an early closing of the sutures of the skull, preventing the brain from developing into the full maturity of the adult European brain.

Scientific racism changed in the mid-nineteenth century with the rise of Darwinian evolutionism. From a more-or-less static hierarchy of races, European racial theorists moved to a picture of races in dynamic struggle, with winners expanding and losers being eliminated from the contest. This was accompanied by a loss of "white" racial self-confidence, and an increased interest in racial "degeneration." One of the key questions for nineteenth-century racial science was that of the high death rates of Europeans in tropical Africa. Was this condition part of a process of environmental adaptation, or was it caused by inherited—and thus immutable—racial traits? If the European inability to survive African conditions was innate, it was not only a specific inferiority of Europeans to Africans, but it also potentially spelled the doom of the entire colonial project. Fear of African diseases also contributed to the social segregation of Africans and Europeans. Europeans were told that excessive contact with Africans would be debilitating. Some also feared that Europeans would "degenerate" in the tropics, as eighteenth-century scientists like De Pauw had spoken of European degeneration in the Americas.

Racial scientists also used science to distinguish between different African peoples. One problem for racists was explaining the fact that some African societies had attained considerably higher levels of cultural achievement, by European standards, than others. These included the building of cities, the production of works of art, and the creation of large-scale societies and polities. Some of these phenomena could be explained as the work of non-African peoples, as the ruins of Great Zimbabwe were explained as the work of ancient Phoenician sailors or the Israelites under King Solomon. But such explanations were of limited use in explaining distinctly African cultural developments. Another possibility was ascribing these developments to a less "African" race, the "Hamitise." Named after Noah's son Ham, the traditional ancestor of the African peoples, the Hamites were usually described as lighter-skinned peoples of extra-African, "Mediterranean," origin, and were credited with many African cultural achievements to the detriment of dark-skinned Africans. The Hamitic theory was principally developed by British scientists but was widely accepted elsewhere. It was often set forth in explicitly racial terms, as the decline of the Hamites was ascribed to the mixture of "Negro blood." Living Africans were sometimes categorized as either "Negroes" or "Hamites." The Belgians distinguished between Negro Hutus and Hamitic Tutsis in Rwanda, helping to cement in place the divisions that would eventually lead to the attempted genocide of the 1990s.

In the twentieth century, the way scientists thought about race was transformed by the introduction of more quantitative ideas. Statistical methods were taking a leap forward in power and rigor, driving a huge range of sciences in the direction of more quantitative analysis. State educational apparatuses were also gaining in the ability to impose classification schemes on their subjects. Standardized testing, particularly the Intelligence Quotient, or "IQ," test promised to provide a "rigorous" system for evaluating the mental capacities of different individuals, and by extension different races and peoples. Intelligence testing spread quickly through Europe and America, and was used both to classify individuals and to make generalizations about races and ethnicities, almost always in favor of the dominant group.

SCIENTIFIC RACISM AND EUGENICS IN COLONIAL SOUTH AFRICA

Scientific racism was particularly powerful in British-ruled South Africa. South Africa was very different from those colonies where a colonial administration simply faced an African population. South Africa, with its long-established white population of "Afrikaner" descendants of Dutch and other European settlers and many British settlers, had the most developed university and college system, popular press, museums, and scientific organizations of any African colony. Darwin's theory of evolution by natural selection was being debated in the South African press as early as the 1870s. The South African Philosophical Society, later the Royal Society of South Africa, was founded in 1877, and began publishing *Transactions* the same year. South Africa, with its wealth and its relatively mild climate was a tempting resort for European scientists, some of whom made new lives there. Rather than simply reading European works or bringing scientists in for short stays, South Africa had the physical anthropologists and ethnologists to classify African peoples and the trained psychologists to develop and administer intelligence tests and evaluate their results. The white population of South Africa also had a considerable degree of self-government within the British Empire.

South Africa was a particularly rich field for physical anthropologists and ethnologists due to the presence of physically and culturally distinct African populations, including the Bushmen, the Khoikhoi, known to the Europeans as "Hottentots," and the majority

Bantu peoples. The first two groups were particularly commonly described as "degenerate" or dying peoples. The developmental history of South Africa was conceptualized in an ascending sequence of races—the Bushmen, the Hottentots, the Bantu, and finally the whites, each an "improvement" on its predecessors. This narrative legitimated white settlement and white control as the carrying out of a long-term historical and evolutionary process by which inferior races were replaced by superior ones.

The situation in South Africa was also complicated by ethnic and class divisions within the white settler population. The principal ethnic division was between the Afrikaners and the more recent British settlers and their descendants. Many Afrikaners had been incorporated into the British Empire by force before and during the South African War from 1899 to 1902 (also known as the "Boer War"). The differences between the two peoples loomed large— until the 1920s the term "race" in South Africa was routinely used to distinguish between Britons and Afrikaners rather than whites and blacks. The South African white population was also more economically diverse than other African settler populations. The country had the continent's only significant population of "poor whites," viewed as biological inferiors by many of the white elite, but an important part of the Afrikaner nation in its confrontations with the British and the indigenous Africans. The presence of a large and diverse white population alongside an even more diverse population of native Africans led many scientists around the world to regard South Africa as a particularly important "laboratory" of racial studies and race relations.

South Africans themselves were aware of the importance of race relations, and many viewed science as providing the answer as to how the races were to live together, and/or how white supremacy was to be justified and maintained. Science was a key aspect of the "European" civilization that many white South Africans prided themselves on being part of. With the latest techniques from Europe, adapted and improved upon by white South Africans themselves, the "race problem" could be scientifically managed rather than being the object of political struggle.

During the late nineteenth and early twentieth centuries, Europe, European colonies, and the Americas were marked by the rise of the "eugenic" movement. Eugenics, literally "good breeding," took many forms, but what eugenicists had in common was encouraging the "superior" elements of the population, usually the upper and middle classes, to reproduce and discouraging the "inferior" elements, usually the working class, the poor, and the "criminal class," from having children. Eugenics drew from social Darwinism and also scientific discoveries about the inability of the environment to affect "genetic" hereditary factors. Many early movements to promote contraception or "family planning," had the eugenic goal of discouraging economically or racially subordinated groups from excessive reproduction. Eugenicists also suggested that some members of the population, especially the "feeble-minded," be sterilized or otherwise prevented from having children.

Eugenics had some followers in South Africa. Many were less concerned with the African population than they were with the poor whites, who they viewed as racial degenerates who should be discouraged from reproducing. However, racism posed a major roadblock to the complete adoption of eugenics in South Africa. There was a strong countervailing trend toward emphasizing white unity against the majority black population, and explaining the "backwardness" of poor whites by environment rather than heredity. Along with the use of intelligence tests to distinguish between races went a reluctance to use them to distinguish between classes within the white population. Many white scientists combined a belief that problems in poor white society were caused by environment with a belief that the relative underdevelopment of black society was caused by heredity.

Distinguishing between races on a scientific basis was an important part of Afrikaner political culture, and several Afrikaner politicians had scientific backgrounds. Hendrik Verwoerd (1901–1966), later the founder of the policy of *apartheid*, or racial separation, and president of independent South Africa, was a professor of applied psychology at the Afrikaner-dominated University of Stellenbosch. However, many were suspicious about using the data created by intelligence testing to make generalizations about the biological and genetic differences of different peoples. They pointed out that tests were created by members of the dominant European culture and that the questions might embody cultural assumptions more difficult for indigenous and uneducated people to grasp.

Racial science was, however, applied to one important issue in South African politics: "miscegenation," interbreeding or sexual intercourse between white and black. Many white leaders, reflecting the consensus of the white community, viewed interracial sex as particularly immoral and dangerous. They claimed that, if unchecked, it would lead to the downfall of the white race in South Africa and create a dangerous population of mixed European and African ancestry, the "coloureds." This condemnation was expressed in the Immorality Act of 1927, which forbade intercourse between whites and Africans outside of marriage, and the Mixed Marriages Act of 1949, which forbade sexual intercourse and marriage between whites and "nonwhites." Supporters of these acts, which came to be seen as pillars of apartheid, called science to the aid of this position, arguing that "mixed bloods" were degenerates both physically and mentally.

The theory of "coloured degeneracy" was upheld by many in the South African intellectual and scientific establishment. Physical anthropologists argued that the mix of African and European traits led to incompatible body parts, such as large African teeth in small European jaws. The zoology professor and comparative anatomist Harold B. Fantham (1876–1937), an immigrant from Britain, collaborated with his wife, the parasitologist Annie Porter, on a series of reports on the "coloured" population. Fantham and Porter, ardent eugenicists, found people of mixed descent both physically inferior to "pure" Europeans and Africans and of poor mental ability and moral character. They lacked the intelligence and energy of the whites, along with the social controls of traditional African society. Fantham was the founder of the Race Welfare Society, a eugenic organization, and was a South African representative to the International Federation of Eugenic Organizations.

THE DECLINE OF SCIENTIFIC RACISM

The decline of scientific racism began in the period following the World War I. The carnage of the war and the seeming inability of European nations to halt the slaughter caused many to question European—and white—superiority.

Another factor leading to the decline of racial science among some scientists was the influence of Marxism. The social and political philosophy originating in the work of Karl Marx (1818–1883) had a particular appeal to some early twentieth-century scientists due to its claim to be a scientific analysis of society. After Russia's Bolshevik Revolution of 1917, some scientists, like many other people, were taken in by a highly distorted picture of the Soviet Union as a technocratic society where central planning by scientifically trained experts was making a better life for all. Marxists, who allied themselves with anticolonial forces in many areas, tended to view class division as the most important phenomenon dividing humanity, with race of decidedly secondary importance, if of any real importance at all. Marxist scientists denied the claims of white supremacists. They viewed white racial science as a "bourgeois" construct, masking the reality of capitalist exploitation of colonized peoples. The Marxist opposition to racism was accentuated in the 1920s by the rise of Italian Fascism and German Nazism, anti-Communist ideologies that emphasized nation and race, particularly in the German case. The virulent racism and anti-Semitism of the Nazis even caused many non-Marxist scientists, particularly those of Jewish descent, to deemphasize innate racial differences.

Economic class was not the only challenger to biological race as a way of classifying Earth's peoples. Race was increasingly giving way to the concept of "culture" as a way to explain and describe human differences. The new "culturalist" approach was embodied in the discipline of cultural anthropology, itself often linked to the desire of colonial administrators to know about the people they were ruling over. Africans were the subject of some of the classic works of anthropology in the early twentieth century, most penned by Europeans and Americans but some written by Africans themselves, such as Jomo Kenyatta (1894–1978) of Kenya. Kenyatta, who became one of Africa's most important anticolonial leaders, wrote *Facing Mount Kenya* (1938), an "ethnography," a study of the customs and culture of his own Gikuyu people, as a thesis at the London School of Economics before it was published as a book.

The decline of scientific racism accelerated during and after the World War II. Nazi Germany and its empire, an attempt (many aspects of which had colonial precedents) to reorder European society on a basis of racial hierarchy, discredited racial thinking both by its failure and by its numberless atrocities. Racial discourse, already declining, ceased to be respectable among scientists as among other people. The new United Nations, founded in 1945 immediately after the war, fostered an ideology of human unity, one that acted against colonialism as well as racism.

Scientific racism faced challenges that emerged within science itself, as well as political ones. The rise of population genetics meant that "races" were increasingly defined as "gene pools," rather than as the "ideal types" of physical anthropology. Between political hostility to the race concept and the rise of population genetics, physical anthropology, despite desperate rearguard actions, was thrust into a crisis from which it has in some ways never recovered.

"ETHNOPSYCHIATRY"

While cultural anthropologists studied African societies in their "natural settings," practitioners of the new science of "ethnopsychiatry" studied individual Africans in more modern settings. Unlike cultural anthropology, ethnopsychiatry emerged in African colonial society itself and it differed from most colonial sciences in that many of its leading practitioners were African settlers or colonial officials, who set the agenda rather than following scientific leaders in Europe or America. It was also more explicitly racist than cultural anthropology, although ethnopsychiatrists, like psychiatrists in general, often wavered between explanations for human behavior based on inherited characteristics and those based on culture and upbringing.

Ethnopsychiatry emerged in African colonies with sizable white settlement, such as French Algeria or British Rhodesia, where whites had extensive experience with Africans not only as colonial subjects, but also as employees. In addition to workshop or entrepreneurial employment, black servants were ubiquitous in white households. Complaining about African servants was an important part of colonial settler culture. Ethnopsychiatry gave a science-based explanation for what white employers viewed as their servants' inadequacies.

Ethnopsychiatrists like J. C. Carothers, a South African who worked mainly in British East Africa, endorsed the already existing stereotype of the African as childlike, with poor impulse control and little capacity for self-denial or the application of general principles, such as cleanliness. Carothers veered between physical explanations based on the alleged peculiarities of the African brain, and explanations based on the inferior qualities of African culture.

Africans, he argued, behaved like those Europeans part of whose forebrains had been destroyed by a process called prefrontal leucotomy. However, he viewed culture as in some degree autonomous, and in some writings presented himself as an antiracist. Carothers became widely recognized in the world psychiatric community as an expert on Africans. The recently founded World Health Organization commissioned him to write a study of African psychology, published as *The African Mind in Health and Disease: A Study in Ethnopsychiatry* (1953). It was widely and favorably reviewed outside Africa.

The ultimate extension of ethnopsychiatry into the political realm was its use to explain African resistance to colonial power. The British government commissioned Carothers to write an analysis of the Kenyan Mau Mau rebellion, which raged from 1952 to 1960, while the French ethnopsychiatrist Octave Mannoni (1899–1989) discussed the Madagascar rebellion against French domination, which took place in 1947 to 1948, in his *Psychologie de Colonisation* (1949). Both the Mau Mau and Madagascar rebellions were repressed with great brutality, although both also paved the way for independence for their respective territories. Carothers and Mannoni explored the rebellions not in terms of the political or economic grievances of the Africans, but in terms of the inadequate African personality. Unlike Carothers, Mannoni viewed African inferiority strictly in cultural rather than physical terms, and turned a harsh light on European settler society as well. He argued that European colonists, after the first generation of explorers and warriors, were driven by an infantile unwillingness to live in a world of equals. Mannoni described the colonial relationship as one of psychological dependence. He explained the Madagascar rebellion as caused not by an actual desire for political independence, which he asserted would not benefit Malagasys, but by an infantile fear of abandonment.

African nationalists vehemently rejected ethnopsychiatry. One of the most influential intellectuals in the anticolonial movement, Frantz Fanon (1925–1961), was a trained psychiatrist himself. Fanon and others attacked the ethnopsychiatrists for their racism and their ignorance of the economic and fundamentally exploitative nature of colonialism. Rather than connecting African mental illness to African biology, Fanon and others charged the colonial system itself with producing mental disorders due to the demands it placed on Africans.

TEACHING SCIENCE IN COLONIAL EDUCATION SYSTEMS

Indigenous African education had its technical aspects. Africans learned the skills necessary in their own societies, as well as the arithmetical skills used in trade. There were also religious schools, whether Islamic madrasas or the schools of the various Christian missionary groups. However, these schools focused on literacy, either in Arabic or in the European language of a missionary group, rather than science. Even at the higher levels, the Christian missions, which dominated much of the educational system in British colonies, focused on religion and humanistic studies rather than science.

In addition, the colonial powers established educational systems in their colonies. These systems were viewed as a way of preparing Africans for "modernization" and economic development and of winning their loyalty toward the colonizing power. On a more pragmatic level, colonial education provided Africans with skills necessary for the colonial governments to function. Not all technical tasks could be given to Europeans. The provision of education was also compatible with the "white man's burden" and "civilizing mission," imperial ideologies that emphasized the service that the imperial power was performing for indigenous peoples.

Educational systems varied greatly among the colonies. At one extreme was the Belgian Congo, which had a widely attended system of elementary education but showed no interest in educating Africans beyond that level. The French and British systems, by contrast, gave higher education to a minority of elite African men, whose loyalty and aid in dealing with ordinary Africans the colonialists hoped to win. A few even attended universities in Europe. The French had more hope than the British of winning the actual loyalty of Africans, although this hope was often frustrated. While the French attempted to integrate educated Africans into the lower levels of colonial administration, the British often distrusted educated Africans, preferring to deal with traditional chiefs and even creating chiefs in African societies originally organized on non-chiefly models. The limited technical and scientific training given to Africans in British colonies tend to focus on the practical needs of administrations. Medical and veterinary education and basic engineering were relatively common, but at independence, African societies had few persons trained in the higher and more theoretical branches of Western science.

Anatomy Class, Sudan. *Frank and Frances Carpenter Collection, Library of Congress (reproduction number LC-USZ62-40645)*

LATE COLONIAL AFRICA AND "EXPERIMENTAL DEVELOPMENTALISM"

In the mid-twentieth century, as European colonial powers faced the challenges of the World Wars and the Great Depression, exploitation of African colonies became a more state-driven activity. Although the colonial state never had the enormous bureaucracies characterizing European states at home, there was a substantial increase in staffing in the post–World War I era and with it in the intrusiveness of colonial power into village communities. Economic exploitation was linked with an ideology of transforming traditional African societies in such a way as to make them both more economically prosperous and greater contributors to the economies of their colonial overlords. These projects for African development were increasingly rhetorically couched as scientific experiments using African societies, people, and economies as experimental subjects. This "research" would eventually lead to the identification of the most productive techniques, which could then be imposed on African societies. This practice is sometimes called "experimental developmentalism."

Arranging entire communities according to experimental protocols required major changes in the lives of the indigenous Africans who were experimental materials. In order for an experiment to produce useful results, conditions had to be rationalized and standardized to the greatest extent possible. Agricultural plots had to be equalized and laid as much as possible in geometric regularity rather than the "irrational" patterns of traditional African land use. Since most experiments were focused on a single crop, indigenous African multicrop agriculture was discouraged or forbidden. There were also attempts to regulate labor by the clock.

Most of these experiments were failures. One of the best-known examples is the "groundnut scheme" in postwar British East Africa. The desperate straits of the British economy after World War II led to plans to more efficiently exploit the colonies to benefit the population of Britain. The "groundnut scheme" was a plan to clear a large area in Tanganyika, Zambia, and Kenya to plant groundnuts (better known in America as peanuts) as a source of vegetable oil. One of the prerequisites was a study of the suitability of the land for cultivation in terms of soil, water supply, and climate. The study took place over a brief period of nine weeks in 1947, not nearly enough time for a proper evaluation of the land. Inadequate scientific preparation was one of the reasons for the failure of the scheme, which cost over £49 million and ruined thousands of acres of land while producing almost nothing. The failure of many such development experiments led to an increased awareness of indigenous expertise in the last decades of colonialism.

SCIENCE AND AFRICAN NATIONALISM IN EARLY POSTCOLONIAL AFRICA

Although colonial authority had always faced resistance from Africans, the twentieth century saw the rise of African nationalist movements that sought to engage colonial authorities and the governments of colonial states politically as well as militarily. The political idioms adopted by these movements varied, but most included a reference to national sovereignty. African nationalists were in a difficult position with regard to science. The usefulness of science and the power of its explanations were undeniable, but Africans had a deep—and mostly warranted—distrust of Western scientific authority, although not many were prepared to go as far as the Indian anticolonial leader Mohandas Gandhi (1869–1948), for whom the rejection of Western science and industrial technology was essential to liberation. Whatever their feelings on science, few African leaders had scientific educations, and African poverty, along with the poor state of African science education, meant that an African scientific elite was slow to develop. The few African scientists continued to rely on foreign funding, educational institutions, and scientific resources.

Elements of continuity included the persistence of scientific and educational institutions established under the colonial regimes, which extended to the retention of European personnel in some cases. European and American scientists also continued to come to Africa to study its unique biological communities. This, however, resulted in a running conflict between scientists wishing to preserve the communities they studied in as pristine a form as possible and African governments wishing to use the land to support their people. Moreover, new institutions established in independent Africa drew on foreign capital and expertise. One example was the International Institute of Tropical Agriculture, founded in Nigeria in 1967 with money from the Ford and Rockefeller foundations. The institute, like other African scientific institutions, employed numerous expatriates from outside the continent and was sometimes perceived by Africans as an alien presence or even imperialists in a new form.

As the African colonies became independent nations in the 1950s and 1960s, there was both continuity and discontinuity in African science. There was also continuity of policy. As was often the case in the immediate aftermath of decolonization, power in much of Africa passed from the hands of colonial administrators into that of a group of Africans with many similarities to the colonial elite. Many had been educated at European universities, and shared the belief of colonial administrators that the culture of ordinary Africans needed to be "modernized," although the new leaders of independent African nations believed that economic development should be directed at creating self-sufficient economies rather than participating in an imperial division of labor. There was a widespread belief among postcolonial elites that scientific and technological development offered a cure for many of the problems that beset independent Africa, such as poverty and disease. Many elements of the experimental developmental culture also persisted into the first decade after independence. African governments continued to think in terms of the big project that would work social and economic transformation on a massive scale in a short time.

One discontinuity between colonial and early national Africa was the declining status of anthropology, suspect due to its connection with colonial administration. The anthropological vision of a "traditional" Africa was resented by nationalists who wanted to encourage modernization. In the universities of independent Africa, it was usually subordinated to sociology, a discipline associated with the study of "modern" as opposed to "traditional" societies, and, particularly in the English-speaking world, with the political left. One exception to this trend was the work of the highly influential Senegalese Cheikh Anta Diop (1923–1986). Trained in France, Diop, who worked at the University of Dakar, used anthropology and linguistics to argue for the profound influence of a "negro" ancient Egypt on other African societies and the ultimately African origins of all human civilization. A "pan-Africanist" in politics, Diop believed that Africa's innate cultural unity should be the foundation of a federal state covering the continent. His linguistic and historical views have had great influence among West African intellectuals and American Afrocentrists, but much less among mainstream students of Africa. Ethnopsychiatry also virtually vanished after African independence.

Although the African scientific community has grown in the decades since independence, African societies still face many difficulties in developing and retaining scientists. None of the world's leading institutions for scientific education is in Africa, and the poverty of the continent along with the wars that have disrupted many of its states have hindered the growth of African science. The "brain drain" of educated Africans to more developed countries, in many cases their old colonial rulers, has also slowed Africa's scientific development.

SOURCES

■ Sir Richard Burton, *First Footsteps in East Africa or a Journey to Harar* (1856)

Richard Francis Burton (1821–1890) was among the greatest of Victorian explorers. He traveled extensively over Asia, the Middle East, Africa, and the Americas. Burton was most renowned in his own time for his journey to Mecca, a city then and now forbidden to non-Muslims. He convincingly disguised himself as an Indian Muslim, a striking testimony to his linguistic and cultural ability. Burton's *First Footsteps in East Africa* is an account of a trip he took after the Meccan journey, to the remote city of Harar in Somaliland—before it became a colony. Burton begins with recounting previous British efforts in the exploration of East Africa, which were carried out from British India by the British East India Company, rather than from Britain itself. East Africa at this time was seen by the British less in the African context and more in that of the western Indian Ocean, along with the Red Sea, South Arabia, and the Persian Gulf. Burton recounts the scientific qualifications and interests of earlier explorers.

As you read this, ask: How did British science relate to exploration and imperialism? Which sciences seem the most important in exploration? How did the interests of colonial administrators, military officers, and a private joint-stock company affect exploration? What appeal was Burton implicitly making to his English readers in this passage?

The project lay dormant until March 1850, when Sir Charles Malcolm[1] and Captain Smyth, President of the Royal Geographical Society of Great Britain, waited upon the chairman of the Court of Directors of the Honourable East India Company.[2] He informed them that if they would draw up a statement of what was required, and specify how it could be carried into effect, the document should be forwarded to the Governor-General of India,[3] with a recommendation that, should no objection arise, either from expense or other causes, a fit person should be permitted to explore the Somali Country.

Sir Charles Malcolm then offered the charge of the expedition to Dr. Carter of Bombay, an officer favourably known to the Indian world by his services on board the "Palinurus" brig[4] whilst employed upon the maritime survey of Eastern Arabia. Dr. Carter at once acceded to the terms proposed by those from whom the project emanated; but his principal object being to compare the geology and botany of the Somali Country with the results of his Arabian travels, he volunteered to traverse only that part of Eastern Africa which lies north of a line drawn

---

[1]Vice Admiral in the Royal Navy since 1847, he had served as superintendent of the Bombay Marine/Indian Navy (see note 6) from 1827 to 1837.

[2]The British joint-stock company that existed under royal charter from December 31, 1600 to January 1, 1874. "John Company," as it was popularly known, administered large areas of India, in the name of the British government until 1858, when the British Crown assumed direct rule over these territories. Burton had served in India as a junior officer in the East India Company's army. Regarding the origins of the East India Company, see the Connections Series book by Glenn Ames, *The Globe Encompassed* (2008), 143–150.

[3]The East India Company's head of administration in India. This post was created by act of Parliament in 1773.

[4]A survey ship of the East India Company, it had explored the Red Sea, as well as eastern Arabia.

from Berberah to Ras Hafun—in fact, the maritime mountains of the Somal. His health not permitting him to be left on shore, he required a cruiser [cruiser][5] to convey him from place to place, and to preserve his store of presents and provisions. By this means he hoped to land at the most interesting points and to penetrate here and there from sixty to eighty miles inland, across the region which he undertook to explore.

On the 17th of August, 1850, Sir Charles Malcolm wrote to Dr. Carter in these terms: "I have communicated with the President of the Royal Geographical Society and others: the feeling is, that though much valuable information could no doubt be gained by skirting the coast (as you propose) both in geology and botany, yet that it does not fulfill the primary and great object of the London Geographical Society, which was, and still is, to have the interior explored." The Vice Admiral, however, proceeded to say that, under the circumstances of the case, Dr. Carter's plans were approved of, and asked him to confer immediately with Commodore Lushington; then Commander in Chief of the Indian Navy.[6]

In May, 1851, Vice Admiral Sir Charles Malcolm died: geographers and travellers lost in him an influential and an energetic friend. During the ten years of his superintendence over the Indian Navy that service rose,[7] despite the incubus of profound peace, to the highest distinction. He freely permitted the officers under his command to undertake the task of geographical discovery, retaining their rank, pay, and batta,[8] whilst the actual expenses of their journeys were defrayed by contingent bills. All papers and reports submitted to the local government were favourably received, and the successful traveller looked forward to distinction and advancement.

Richard Burton, *First Footsteps in East Africa or a Journey to Harar* (Koln: Konemann, 1990), 9–11.

■ Karl Peters, *The Eldorado of the Ancients* (1902)

Karl Peters (1856–1918) was the leading German African explorer and promoter of German colonization in Africa. Like other promoters, he emphasized the economic potential of Africa and the possibilities of enriching the home country through exploiting it. As a colonialist, Peters was devoted to German interests and had little regard or concern for

---

[5]Here he probably means a small yacht, as opposed to a warship.
[6]Also known as the Bombay Marine, it served as the East India Company's navy from 1613 to 1863.
[7]See note 1.
[8]The extra allowance given to East India officers serving in India and surrounding waters.

the indigenous inhabitants. He was discharged from his position as Commissioner of German East Africa in 1897 for his cruelty to native Africans. The following passage from *The Eldorado of the Ancients,* a work combining Peters's experiences in Africa with an archeological argument that southern Africa had been the source of gold for the ancient world, discusses the meteorological cycle in the valley of the Zambezi river. How does Peters expect European know-how to change the Zambezi? How does he contrast European with African society in terms of science? What relation might the technological transformation of the Zambezi have to the imperial projects Peters was devoted to?

On the Zambesi the rains come to an end towards the beginning of April, in July the crops are reaped, in August the grass begins to get scorched, and then the country is exposed to the burning Sun, black and still as a corpse. The river-beds grow dry. Even the Zambesi is changed from a mighty stream into a number of shallow rivulets, which, for all that, are still navigable by small boats. The water-holes are empty, and the natives must often walk daily for hours to supply their need of the indispensable element. There is no question but that, even during these months, water is everywhere obtainable underground, and that European science would easily succeed in revolutionising the country in this respect. But, for the present, it is the negro who counts here, and the negro is not fond of revolutions, least of all scientific ones. Thus, the land grows more and more dry; and bleak and waste, as in winter-time with us, the greater part of the landscape stretches before one's eyes, with this difference certainly, that such evergreen trees as palms, acacias, mitondos, and aloes still put a certain variety into the picture. In September, and even more so in October, the heat becomes sultry and almost unbearable. The temperature rises to 113 [degrees] Fahr[enheit] in the shade by day, and the nights, although considerably cooler, often bring no real relief.

Carl Peters, *The Eldorado of the Ancients* (New York: Dutton, 1902), 77.

■ **E. B. Worthington,** *Science in Africa: A Review of Scientific Research Relating to Tropical and Southern Africa* **(1938)**

The African Research Survey was a program of research and organization to determine how the people of Africa could be more effectively governed and the continent's resources could be more productively exploited. Although the people who carried out the survey and reported on the results were British, the effort was funded by an American philanthropy, the Carnegie Foundation. Edgar B. Worthington's *Science in Africa* was a report on part of this effort. (Other works commissioned alongside Worthington's examined Africa's peoples and its economy.) It covered a broad range of scientific problems including agriculture, education, and scientific organization. Worthington was not afraid to criticize what he viewed as the mistaken policies of colonial governments.

Worthington was a young biologist trained at Cambridge University, with a particular interest in ecology. In this passage, he discusses the role of science in agricultural "improvement." According to Worthington, what has been the greatest hindrance to agricultural improvement to this point, and how does he propose to correct that error? What part does Worthington see scientific research playing in the colonial enterprise? How is scientific knowledge to be applied, and what is the role of indigenous African people? What is the role of colonial administrators in furthering scientific agriculture? How does Worthington attempt to distinguish the British Empire from other colonial empires?

To the native peoples, agriculture is an essential part of tribal life and innovations are resisted through attachment to customary methods and sometimes also through the influence of religious and magical belief. In the past the enforcement of radical changes in native methods has been advocated, but in recent years native agricultural practice has been regarded as worthy of respect. It is now coming to be realized that drastic methods rarely achieve their object, and that improvements are more likely to be attained by gradual development from existing methods. The first step is to understand these methods and their reasons, just has been done in the study of agricultural science in Europe during the past fifty years. Native methods are then submitted to scientific analysis and experiment, and improvements, when discovered, are encouraged through the medium of demonstration farms and other forms of education. The procedure may not be applicable to exotic crops such as cotton, coffee, or cacao, which are new to the native peoples. In such cases, the native has to be taught methods which are likely to be successful in his hands from the beginning.

In applying new or improved methods among native agriculturalists, a major question is whether or not some form of compulsion is justified or even effective. As a rule, in British territories, every effort is made to avoid compulsion, but there are certain cases where it appears to be justified. For example, when a new crop of known value and suitability is to be introduced in an area, some compulsion in the initial stages may be the only way of demonstrating to the farmers the advantages which they themselves can derive from its cultivation. Again, in the control of certain pests and diseases, measures may have to be enforced on all farmers, irrespective of race, in order to protect the careful farmer from his neighbour's neglect. Such cases are covered by agricultural pests and disease ordinances. In certain colonies, moreover, compulsory measures against soil erosion, made applicable to natives, may have resulted in a greater advance in the lay-out of native than of non-native farms. In the opinion of some authorities the only way to make real advance in some forms of indigenous agriculture is by compulsion on a large scale, as in the compulsory system employed with success in the Congo[9] . . . and the proposed compulsory culling of stock to reduce over-grazing in East Africa. If it is possible to generalize about so complicated a question, it may be claimed that at least in British territories it is the aim to improve native methods by education and only to employ compulsion where all else has failed. In some non-British territories direct compulsion is more often used, with the consequence that results are produced more rapidly and more cheaply, but perhaps they are not so satisfactory in the long run.

   It is a simple truth, realized by all concerned, that the principal factor retarding native agricultural improvement is a lack of a balanced knowledge concerning conditions of native life. Modern anthropology helps to fill this gap, but for the practical advances in view recent work in this field does not appear always to lay sufficient stress on the material background of man's environment. There is general agreement as to the importance of agricultural advance among Africans, as a basis for general improvements in the standard of living; but before native agriculture is improved we must have a sound knowledge of existing conditions.

E. B. Worthington, *Science in Africa: A Review of Scientific Research Relating to Tropical and Southern Africa* (London: Oxford University Press, 1938), 303–304. By permission of Oxford University Press.

■ Frantz Fanon, *The Wretched of the Earth* (1961)

Psychiatrist Frantz Fanon was born in the Caribbean French colony of Martinique. After medical training in France, he began to work as a psychiatrist in Algeria, then a French colony undergoing a violent

---

[9]The Belgian Congo, which King Leopold II relinquished to his nation's control in 1908.

conflict between French authorities and an independence movement. Strongly anti-colonial, Fanon wrote several books on the psychology of colonialism and independence movements. In them he attacked white "ethnopsychiatrists" like J. C. Carothers and Octave Mannoni, whose work he found racist and corrupted by its support of colonialism. Fanon's case histories emphasized the damage done to the psyche of Africans by colonialism.

The following passage from his most famous work, *Les Damnés de la Terre*, introduces a collection of case histories of mentally ill Algerians and French people resident in Algeria. How does Fanon see the relationship of colonial control over nature and colonial politics? How does he distinguish between "successful colonization" and the period of the independence struggle? How does he connect colonialism and the mental health of the colonized?

Hostile nature, obstinate and fundamentally rebellious, is in fact represented in the colonies by the bush, by mosquitoes, natives, and fever, and colonization is a success when all this indocile nature has finally been tamed. Railways across the bush, the draining of swamps, and a native population which is non-existent politically and economically are in fact one and the same thing.

In the period of colonization when it is not contested by armed resistance, when the sum total of harmful nervous stimuli overstep a certain threshold, the defensive attitudes of the natives give way and they then find themselves crowding the mental hospitals. There is thus during the calm period of successful colonization a regular and important mental pathology which is the direct product of oppression.

Today the war of national liberation which has been carried on by the Algerian people for the last seven years has become a favorable breeding ground for mental disorders, because so far as the Algerians are concerned it is a total war. We shall mention here some Algerian cases which have been attended by us and who seem to us to be particularly eloquent. We need hardly say that we are not concerned with producing a scientific work. We avoid all arguments over semiology,[10] nosology,[11] or therapeutics.[12] The few technical terms used serve merely as references. We must, however, insist on two points. Firstly, as a general rule, clinical psychiatry classifies the different disturbances

---

[10]The branch of medical science concerned with symptoms.
[11]The classification or arrangement of diseases.
[12]The remedial treatment of disease.

shown by our patients under the heading "reactionary psychoses." In doing this, prominence is given to the event which has given rise to the disorder, although in some cases mention is made of the previous history of the case (the psychological, affective, and biological condition of the patient) and of the type of background from whence he comes. It seems to us that in the cases here chosen, the events giving rise to the disorder are chiefly the bloodthirsty and pitiless atmosphere, the generalization of inhuman practices, and the firm impression that people have of being caught up in a veritable Apocalypse.

Epilogue: Making Connections: How Much Have Things Changed?

How can we locate and describe science in the modern world? One point is that the scientific tradition of the West has maintained and even expanded its dominant position, with roots in the Scientific Revolution and the Colonial Age. Indeed, throughout much of the world, Western science is simply "science," as other scientific traditions have been marginalized or have entirely disappeared. However, Western science has also become less "Western" (namely European and North American), with new centers of science emerging in East and South Asia, as well as Latin America.

Science has also become a global force. Few human societies have remained untouched by it. Science occupies a major part of the curriculum at educational institutions across the globe, and politicians and ordinary people watch with anxious care the rankings of their country's students in scientific knowledge and take pride in its scientific achievements. Millions of scientists in a wide variety of disciplines are employed in countries throughout the world. Both popular and technical books on science sell widely, and thousands of academic journals, newspapers, popular magazines, and web sites disseminate to an eager global audience the latest scientific discoveries. In addition, science fiction is a popular genre of entertainment.

Many of the issues explored in this book remain important. The direct descendants of the medieval university continue to be centers of scientific research and education, and have spread to cover the world. Science plays a vastly more important role in the modern curriculum than it did in the European Middle Ages. The relationship between the West and the Islamic world has also been reversed, in that now Islamic societies are forced to adopt, willingly or unwillingly, the science developed in other civilizations. Muslims working in the Western tradition, such as 1979 Nobel Prize for Physics co-winner Abdus Salam (1926–1996), have produced some important science, and form a significant percentage of persons working in Western universities and other scientific centers. However, Islamic countries themselves have not been scientific leaders.

Although religious orders are no longer the creative force in science that they were in the great age of Jesuit science, the issues of religion and science that Jesuits like Ricci and Kircher grappled with remain crucial to modern culture. While the Jesuits were faced with the challenge of heliocentrism, religious believers today throughout the Jewish, Christian, and Islamic worlds are faced with the apparent contradictions between the creation accounts in their sacred texts and Charles Darwin's theory of evolution through natural selection and the findings of modern cosmology. Although Western science is not usually presented nowadays, as it was by the Jesuits, as part of a "package" with Western religion, non-Western societies are still faced with the choice of how much Western culture to accept along with science. The kind of research agenda that led to the discovery of quinine's power over malaria has its successor in the "bioprospecting" for wonder drugs in nature now carried on not by religious groups, but by multinational corporations, whose global reach challenges and even exceeds that of the Jesuits of old.

Peter the Great's Russia and Shogun Yoshimune's Japan have been followed by a legion of countries seeking to take the knowledge of Western science and use it for the agendas of their rulers. Science has proven compatible with authoritarian rule in many places, and "modernizing" dictators like Iraq's Saddam Hussein have found scientists to serve them. As it was in Peter's day, military needs often drive the growth of science in both "advanced" and "less developed" countries. One of the most notorious scientists in the world is

Pakistani nuclear researcher Abdul Qadeer Khan (born 1936) associated both with Pakistan's successful attempt to develop a nuclear weapon and the dissemination of nuclear technology to North Korea, Libya, and Iran. Despite the successes of authoritarian regimes like Pakistan's, the most scientifically advanced countries in the twentieth and twenty-first centuries have been democracies like the United States, Western Europe, and Japan. Authoritarian China, though, may be challenging that position of preeminence in the coming decades.

Although the kind of direct colonialism practiced by the European powers in the nineteenth and twentieth centuries has vanished from the African continent and most of the rest of the world, global imbalances of power continue to shape the scientific agenda. "Third world" scientists and organizations have advocated for a reorientation of science to serve the needs of the world's poor, but with little success. Leaders of formerly colonized countries, such as South Africa's President Thabo Mbeki (born 1942), have often demonstrated suspicion of Western science, in part caused by its colonial associations. Mbeki's questioning of the scientific consensus on the causes and treatment of the AIDS infection and his exaltation of traditional African medicine demonstrate that science's colonial legacy continues to shape its reception.[1]

SCIENCE AND THE WORLD'S FUTURE

Science will remain vitally important for the global community for the foreseeable future. Many of the most important problems of modern society can be solved only with the aid of science, from the AIDS epidemic to the loss of oceanic resources. One of the best-known world problems of our time is "global warming," which by its name indicates that it is not a problem of a single region but of the entire world. Both global warming and contemporary science are products of modern, industrial civilization. However, science is not only essential for observing, defining, and demonstrating the problem, but also for solving it, if there is a solution.

But the destructive as well as constructive power of science will shape the future. The terrifying weapons of the twentieth century—

---

[1]See "A Modern Plague: AIDS in Sub-Saharan Africa, 1982 to the Present," in the Connections Series book by John Aberth, *The First Horseman: Disease in Human History* (2007), 115–154.

the atomic and hydrogen bombs, the "designer germs" of biological warfare laboratories—are as much products of science as cheap power and abundant food. Great scientific projects that seem carefully thought-out and well-intentioned, like the groundnuts scheme in British colonial Africa, can backfire with catastrophic consequences to the Earth's fragile ecology. Like the future of the world, the future of science remains unknown. However, we can be sure that its future will build on its past.

Bibliography

USEFUL WORKS ON THE HISTORY OF WORLD SCIENCE

The world history of science is a field that is just beginning to develop. Toby E. Huff's *The Rise of Early Modern Science: Islam, China and the West* (1995) is a controversial comparative study by a sociologist, which argues that the West was able to catch up and surpass the previously dominant scientific traditions of China and the Islamic world due to its unique cultural and social institutions. Harold J. Cook's *Matters of Exchange* (2007) attempts to put the Scientific Revolution of the seventeenth century into a global context by examining its relation to the Dutch global trade network. Peter Bowler's *The Norton History of the Environmental Sciences* (1993) is a treatment of the sciences that take the world for their subject, including geology, meteorology, botany, and zoology. There is much relevant to the history of science in John Aberth's Connections Series book, *The First Horseman: Disease in Human History* (2007).

The area of world science that has received the most attention is the relation of science to modern European imperialism. A collection edited by Roy McLeod, *Nature and Empire: Science and the Colonial Enterprise* (2000) contains several excellent essays. One specialized collection is Londa Schiebinger and Claudia Swan's *Colonial Botany: Science, Commerce and Politics in the Early Modern World* (2005). Richard H. Grove's *Green Imperialism: Colonial Expansion, Tropical Island Edens and the Origins of Environmentalism, 1600–1860* (1995) explores the relationship of global imperialism and environmental science.

A recent study of some of the environmental disasters that have occurred due to mismanaged technology around the globe is Andrew L. Jenks's Connections Series book, *Perils of Progress: Environmental Disasters in the Twentieth Century* (2010).

USEFUL WORKS ON MEDIEVAL SCIENCE

There are numerous general studies of medieval science in both the Islamic and the Latin Christian worlds. Howard R. Turner's *Science in Medieval Islam: An Illustrated Introduction* (1997) is a good survey, with a particularly fine set of illustrations of scientific instruments. Seyyed Hossein Nasr's *Science and Civilization in Islam* (1968, rev. ed. 1987) treats Islamic science as an aspect of Islamic civilization, rather than as a chapter of the history of science. It contains numerous lengthy extracts in translation from the writings of Muslim scientists. George Saliba's *Islamic Science and the Making of the European Renaissance* (2007) is a controversial revisionist interpretation, dating both the rise and the decline of Islamic science over a much longer period of time than have many previous scholars. The continuing influence of Islamic science on Western thought after the Middle Ages is the subject of Nancy Siraisi's *Avicenna in Renaissance Italy: The Canon and Medical Teaching in Italian Universities after 1500* (1987).

The literature on science in the European Middle Ages is voluminous. An old but good book is by A.C. Crombie: *Science in the Middle Ages, 5th to 13th Centuries* (1969). Edward Grant's *The Foundations of Modern Science in the Middle Ages: Their Religious, Institutional, and Intellectual Contexts* (1996) is a very useful introduction to the subject of science in the world of medieval Latin Christianity, focusing on institutions and practices rather than the development of scientific ideas themselves. In the history of specific disciplines, Siraisi's *Medieval and Early Renaissance Medicine: An Introduction to Knowledge and Practice* (1990) and Grant's *Planets, Stars, and Orbs: The Medieval Cosmos, 1200–1687* (1994) are both excellent.

USEFUL WORKS ON JESUIT SCIENCE

There is no book covering the full range of Jesuit scientific activities in the early modern period. The collections *The Jesuits: Cultures, Sciences and the Arts, 1540–1773* (1999) and *The Jesuits II: Cultures, Sciences and Arts 1540–1773* (2006), edited by John W. O'Malley, Gauvin Alexander Bailey, Stephen J. Harris, and T. Frank Kennedy, however, contain many stimulating essays on Jesuit science.

The Jesuit experience in China has attracted a great deal of attention. Jonathan Spence's *The Memory Palace of Matteo Ricci* (1984) discusses Ricci's science in the context of his general missionary effort. Liam Matthew Brockey's *Journey to the East: The Jesuit Mission to China, 1579–1724* (2007) is a voluminous study with much to say about Jesuit science. Spence and Brockey write mainly from the Jesuit point of view; a good complement to their books is Benjamin A. Elman's *On Their Own Terms: Science in China, 1550–1900* (2005), which deals with the Jesuit impact (and that of the Protestant missionaries of the nineteenth century) from the point of view of Chinese intellectual history.

The most recent biography of José de Acosta in English is Claudio Burguleta's *José de Acosta* (1999). It emphasizes Acosta's European Jesuit background and concern with the Catholic religious mission in Spanish America. A good counterbalance is Antonio Barrera-Osorio's *Experiencing Nature: The Spanish American Empire and the Early Scientific Revolution* (2006), which focuses on imperial needs and the scientific community in Mexico and Peru. The eighteenth-century debate on the New World, which involved many Jesuits and ex-Jesuits, is exhaustively discussed in Antonello Gerbi's *The Dispute of the New World: History of a Polemic, 1750–1900* (1973).

Athanasius Kircher has been the subject of increased interest in recent years. A collection edited by Paula Findlen, *Athanasius Kircher: The Last Man Who Knew Everything* (2004) is a good place to start.

USEFUL WORKS ON SCIENCE IN TOKUGAWA JAPAN AND ROMANOV RUSSIA

Masayoshi Sugimoto and David L. Swain's *Science and Culture in Traditional Japan A.D. 600–1854* (1978) is a good introduction to the history of pre-Meiji Japanese science, stressing the impact of successive "waves" of Chinese and Western science. James R. Bartholomew's *The Formation of Science in Japan: Building a Research Tradition* (1989) focuses on the Meiji period but has an interesting discussion of the Tokugawa background and the transition to the much more Western-influenced science of Meiji. Its sociological and institutional focus complements Sugimoto and Swain's intellectual and cultural one. Few *rangaku* works are available in English. One exception is Sugita Genpaku's *Dawn of Western Science in Japan* (1969), the title of which would be more accurately translated as *The Beginnings of Dutch Studies*, a short autobiographical account by a Japanese physican and translator. Donald Keene's *The Japanese Discovery of Europe, 1720–1830* (rev. ed. 1969) discusses many Japanese writers both in and out of the *rangaku* movement. Ellen Gardner Nakamura's *Practical Pursuits: Takano Choei, Takahashi Keisaku, and Western Medicine in Nineteenth-century Japan* (2005) is a fascinating study of how some Japanese physicians adopted Western medicine in the late Tokugawa era.

There is less available in English on early modern Russian science. James Cracraft's *The Petrine Revolution in Russian Culture* (2004) treats the cultural transformation Peter the Great wrought, with extensive discussion of science and technology. Cracraft is an unabashed admirer of the tsar. An older book, but still quite useful, is Alexander Vucinich's *Science in Russian Culture, A History to 1860* (1963), the first part of a two-volume history of science under the Czars. A good source for the ideas of nineteenth-century Russian liberals about science is Alexander Herzen's *Selected Philosophical Works* (1956). Some more recent cases of "modernization from above" are the subject of Cyrus Veeser's Connections book, *Great Leaps Forward: Modernizers in Africa, Asia and Latin America* (2009).

USEFUL WORKS ON SCIENCE IN COLONIAL AND EARLY NATIONAL AFRICA

There is no overall study of science in colonial Africa. A collection edited by Helen L. Tilley with Robert J. Gordon, *Ordering Africa:*

Anthropology, European Imperialism and the Politics of Knowledge (2007) contains several useful studies of the human sciences in British, French, Italian, and German Africa. Paul F. Cranefield's *Science and Empire: East Coast Fever in Rhodesia and the Transvaal* (1991) is an exhaustive, tightly focused study of one disease of livestock and the British government and scientific establishment's response to it. Thomas Bass's *Camping with the Prince and Other Tales of Science in Africa* (1990) collects fascinating stories of encounters with scientists and scientific institutions in independent Africa in a very readable fashion.

Africa appears in several general studies of colonial science. Michael Osborne's *Nature, the Exotic, and the Science of French Colonialism* (1994) is a study of the French Empire of the nineteenth century through the lens of attempts to acclimate useful plants and animals in the empire to France. Osborne's focus on the life sciences is complemented by Lewis Pyenson's *Civilizing Mission: Exact Sciences and French Overseas Expansion, 1830–1940* (1993), which concentrates on meteorology, astronomy and geodesy. Richard Drayton's *Nature's Government: Science, Imperial Britain, and the 'Improvement' of the World* (2000) examines the relation of science and imperialism in the eighteenth and nineteenth-century British Empire.

The literature on scientific racism is vast. Londa Schiebinger's *Nature's Body: Gender in Making of Modern Science* (1993) deals with the origin of scientific racism in the eighteenth century. A classic with a nineteenth and early twentieth century focus is Stephen Jay Gould's *The Mismeasure of Man* (1981). Elazar Barkan, *The Retreat of Scientific Racism: Changing Concepts of Race in Britain and the United States between the Wars* (1992) covers the changes of the mid-twentieth century. A good local African study is Saul Dubrow's *Scientific Racism in Modern South Africa* (1995), which despite its title is about the first half of the twentieth century. Jock McCulloch's *Colonial Psychiatry and the "African Mind"* (1995) traces the development of ethnopsychiatry.

DOCUMENTARY SOURCES

Medieval Documents

Adelard of Bath and Berechiah ha-Nakdan, *Dodi Ve-Nechdi*, ed. and trans. H. Gollancz London. Oxford University Press, 1920.

Ibn Rushd, Abu'l Walid Muhammad. *The Philosophy and Theology of Averroes*, trans. Mohammed Jamil-al-Rahman. Baroda: A. G. Widgery, 1921.

Prologue to Leon Joseph of Carcassonne's Hebrew translation of Gerard de Solo's *Practica super nono Almansoris* from Luis Garcia-Ballester, Lola Ferre, and Eduard Feliu, "Jewish Appreciation of Fourteenth-Century Scholastic Medicine" *Osiris* 6 (1990): 106–114.

Oliver Joseph Thatcher, ed. *The Library of Original Sources*. Milwaukee: University Research Extension, 1915.

Jesuit Documents

Acosta, José de. *Natural and Moral history of the Indies, by Father Joseph de Acosta. Reprinted from the English translated edition of Edward Grimston, 1604. And ed., with notes and an introduction, by Clements R. Markham.* Two Volumes. London: Hakluyt Society, 1880.

Ricci, Matteo. *The True Meaning of the Lord of Heaven (T'ien-chu Shih-i).* Translated with Introduction and Notes by Douglas Lancashire and Peter Hu Kuo-chen, S. J., edited by Edward J. Malatesta, S. J., St. Louis: The Institute of Jesuit Sources in cooperation with the Ricci Institute, 1985.

Rodrigues, Joao. *Joao Rodrigues's Account of Sixteenth-Century Japan.* Michael Cooper, ed. London: Hakluyt Society, 2001.

The volcano's, or, Burning and fire-vomiting mountains famous in the world, with their remarkables collected for the most part out of Kircher's Subterraneous world; and exposed to more general view in English . . ., London: Printed by J. Darby for John Allen . . . 1669.

Japanese and Russian Documents

Dashkova, Ekaterina. *Memoirs of the Princess Daschkaw, Lady of Honour to Catherine II* translated by W. Bradford. Two volumes. London: Henry Colburn, 1840.

Japan and the Japanese in the Nineteenth Century. London: John Murray, 1852.

Keene, Donald. *The Japanese Discovery of Europe.* Rev. ed. Stanford: Stanford University Press, 1969.

Staehlin von Storcksberg, Jakob. *Original Anecdotes of Peter the Great,* London, 1788.

African Documents

Burton, Richard F. *First Footsteps in East Africa, or, an Exploration of Harar.* 1856. Reprint 2000. Koln: Konemann Verlagsgeschellschaft mbH.

Fanon, Frantz. *The Wretched of the Earth.* Translated by Constance Farrington. New York: Grove Press, 1963.

Peters, Carl. *The Eldorado of the Ancients.* New York: Dutton, 1902.

Worthington, E. B. *Science in Africa: A Review of Scientific Research Relating to Tropical and Southern Africa.* Oxford University Press, 1938. Reprint 1969. Negro Universities Press.

Index

Note: Page numbers followed by n indicate notes. Italicized page numbers refer to primary source documents.